MW00529205

ADVANCE PRAISE FOR *A SEARCH FOR COMMON GROUND*

"One of the great challenges in education improvement today is how often our political fights and ideological polarization get in the way of doing what's best for kids. Rick and Pedro perform a civil service wading into our toughest educational disputes and show that respectful engagement can surface principled common ground."

—Governor **Jeb Bush**, founder and chair, ExcelinEd

"We are stronger, and smarter, when we work together. We reach better results when we listen to one another. This courageous conversation about how we leverage and work through our differences of opinion to produce meaningful improvements for students, families, and educators is a template for our nation and for school communities all across the United States. If we commit to the work of respecting one another enough to listen and learn, as Dr. Noguera and Dr. Hess have done here, we can indeed break through the polarization that too often hampers our progress and create a better system for learning in our country."

—Governor **Michelle Lujan Grisham**

"If you despair that our public schools are beyond repair, read this book. If you despair that people of widely divergent views can no longer debate them without rancor, read this book. (If neither of these thoughts are bothering you, do a little homework and then read it!)"

—Governor **Mitch Daniels**, president, Purdue University

"When it comes to education, Americans agree much more than our polarized political rhetoric would suggest—and where they disagree, they can still find civil ways to speak across their differences. That's precisely what Rick Hess and Pedro Noguera demonstrate in this sharp and perceptive book. Let's hope the rest of us can follow their example."

—**Jonathan Zimmerman**, professor of history of education, University of Pennsylvania

"This is a book for our times: a back-and-forth between two leading thinkers on important, complicated education policy issues. Its real value, beyond its content, is the way Rick and Pedro engage to learn. By sharing experiences and data, delving deeply to understand each other's motivations, and seeking areas of agreement without papering over disagreements, they model the policy conversations we need today."

—**Rajiv Vinnakota**, president, Institute for Citizens and Scholars

"It's nice to read an exchange between two leading scholars on the issues education leaders must contend with. Thoughtful and engaging, readers will find this book useful for understanding the complex challenges facing schools today."

—**Austin Beutner**, superintendent, Los Angeles Unified School District

"This book is a master class in breaking through the silos that polarize education reform and breaking down why they exist in the first place. It should be required reading for any education leader, graduate student, or parent who seeks to understand the complexity of school improvement. It weaves political philosophy, politics, and the perils of implementation together in an infinitely readable volume."

—**Celine Coggins**, executive director, Grantmakers for Education

"We don't agree on everything—and that is the point of this book. We can have vigorous debates, see each other's perspectives, learn from the conversation, and, where possible, find common ground to advance excellence and equity for kids."

—**Elisa Villanueva Beard**, CEO, Teach for America

A Search for Common Ground

Conversations About the Toughest Questions in K–12 Education

Frederick M. Hess
Pedro A. Noguera

TEACHERS COLLEGE PRESS

TEACHERS COLLEGE | COLUMBIA UNIVERSITY
NEW YORK AND LONDON

Published by Teachers College Press®, 1234 Amsterdam Avenue, New York, NY 10027

Copyright © 2021 by Teachers College, Columbia University

Cover photo by esseffe / iStock by Getty Images.

All rights reserved. No part of this publication may be reproduced or transmitted in any form or by any means, electronic or mechanical, including photocopy, or any information storage and retrieval system, without permission from the publisher. For reprint permission and other subsidiary rights requests, please contact Teachers College Press, Rights Dept.: tcpressrights@tc.columbia.edu

Library of Congress Cataloging-in-Publication Data

Names: Hess, Frederick M., author. | Noguera, Pedro, author.
Title: A search for common ground : conversations about the toughest
   questions in K–12 education / Frederick M. Hess, Pedro A. Noguera.
Description: New York, NY : Teachers College Press, [2021] |
   Includes bibliographical references and index.
Identifiers: LCCN 2020054599 (print) | LCCN 2020054600 (ebook) |
   ISBN 9780807765166 (paperback) | ISBN 9780807765173 (hardcover) |
   ISBN 9780807779477 (ebook)
Subjects: LCSH: Communication in politics—United States. | Political culture—
   United States. | School improvement programs—United States.
Classification: LCC JA85.2.U6 H47 2021 (print) | LCC JA85.2.U6 (ebook) |
   DDC 370.973—dc23
LC record available at https://lccn.loc.gov/2020054599
LC ebook record available at https://lccn.loc.gov/2020054600

ISBN 978-0-8077-6516-6 (paper)
ISBN 978-0-8077-6517-3 (hardcover)
ISBN 978-0-8077-7947-7 (ebook)

Printed on acid-free paper
Manufactured in the United States of America

For Gray and Blake: May your schools be palaces of learning, imagination, and beauty—and may the work of creating such schools summon forth the better angels in each of us.

−R. H.

I dedicate this book to my youngest daughter, Ava, and my grandchildren: Ashe, Shanti, Imani, and Vicente. In my family they represent the future generation, and my hope is that they will have the compassion, courage, and creativity to address the problems they will inherit from my generation.

−P. N.

Contents

Acknowledgments

We're deeply indebted to the many people who helped bring this unusual volume to life. First and foremost, we'd like to offer our profound thanks to the terrifically talented triumvirate of R. J. Martin, Tracey Schirra, and Hannah Warren for their invaluable editing and indispensable support. They helped sharpen our thoughts and supported this project in all manner of ways. We couldn't have done this without them. We owe additional thanks to Hayley Sanon, Matt Rice, and Jessica Schurz for all their help in bringing this unusual project to fruition.

We were fortunate to benefit from the thoughtful suggestions of so many friends and colleagues. But we owe extra thanks to those special few who were kind enough to read an earlier version of the manuscript and provide incisive feedback: Alex Baron, Brendan Bell, Howard Blume, Derrell Bradford, Laura Desimone, Max Eden, Carl Glickman, Kaya Henderson, Julia Rafal-Baer, Elizabeth Rich, Ian Rowe, Stefanie Sanford, Carolyn Sattin-Bajaj, Esa Syeed, and Jonathan Zimmerman.

We are both privileged to work at institutions that give us the intellectual freedom to pursue an endeavor of this kind, without constraints or qualifications. As ever, Rick owes the deepest appreciation to the American Enterprise Institute (AEI) and its president, Robert Doar, for the support that makes this work possible and for providing a cherished home for nearly two decades. AEI is committed to the robust, healthy competition of ideas, and this book is a study in the kind of vigorous exchange that can help bring that vision to life.

Pedro would similarly like to thank his colleagues at the University of California, Los Angeles, and the University of Southern California (USC). When we started this project, Pedro was on the faculty in the Graduate School of Information Studies at UCLA, and by the time we completed the writing, he was the new dean at the Rossier School of

Education at USC. Both UCLA and USC have been extremely supportive of his work and have provided the time and space required for this
endeavor.

We also want to offer special thanks to the talented team at Teachers
College Press. We've both had the privilege of working with TCP for
many years, and the relationship is one we've found both personally
and professionally rewarding. We want to offer particular thanks to
Brian Ellerbeck, TCP's executive acquisitions editor and the man who
helped Rick first conceptualize the idea for this book. We're grateful to
Brian and his team for both their suggestions and unwavering enthusiasm for this project.

And although we're grateful to all those who've helped us out along
the way, we owe a special thanks to our loving families for tolerating
our fevered scribblings in the midst of a pandemic and shutdown—
even when it meant we were half-distracted while dealing with the
inevitable household crises that accompany the boisterous presence of
young children.

Lastly, it should go without saying that any and all mistakes, flaws,
and inanities in the pages that follow are ours and ours alone.

Preface

In this angry era, we spend a lot of time arguing, trading barbs, and disputing facts.

That's not what this book is about. If you picked it up seeking snarky asides or devastating put-downs, you're going to be disappointed. Honestly, there's plenty of that available already. That's not what we've tried to do here.

We've set out to do something more difficult and, we think, more urgent. Our aim was to better understand one another and why we think about education the way that we do. In that respect, this book is probably best understood as something that we've found all too rare of late: an exercise in listening and learning.

In late 2019, when we started to explore this project, we talked about the division and frustration that have become all too familiar in America today. We discussed the posturing and distrust that are rife in education and how hard all of this makes it to sort through complicated issues or to find common ground.

Part of this, we suspected, was simply a function of how the world works today. Social media and 24/7 news cycles make it hard to engage in sustained, patient conversation. Like everyone else in this connected world, educators, scholars, and advocates tend to rush from one thing to the next—from email to text messages to meetings to their news feed—with little time for reflection or sustained back-and-forth.

When training educators, we talk a lot about the need for "courageous conversations." We fear, however, that we have too few of these in practice. The truth is, there's nothing courageous about preaching to the choir. It's not courageous for liberals to tell one another that they're right or for conservatives to do the same. Courageous conversations require sitting down with those who see, think, and feel differently and then being willing to listen—not lecture.

Listening is hard. Trust us, we get it. We've spent much of the past few decades on opposing sides of important educational debates, with Pedro generally on the Left and Rick mostly on the Right. Although we have a lot of respect for each other, we also view important questions in very different ways. We're both old enough to have developed pretty strong convictions over decades of research, writing, speaking, and teaching, and that means it's easy to lapse into familiar sound bites. It can be terribly difficult to break that pattern. But it's possible.

And it turns out breaking that pattern is a lot easier when you're not worried about squeezing a rejoinder into a Twitter post or reacting in real time to the latest outrage. It's easier when you have the time to go back and forth, and process what has been said.

In fact, the format here probably deserves as much credit as either of us for whatever value this book holds. The chapters in this volume skip from one contentious education conversation to the next, with each unfolding as an exchange spanning a number of letters. As we corresponded, we were reminded of just what's been lost with the disappearance of the letter-writing culture. There's unique power in that kind of deliberate, sustained exchange of ideas.

James Baldwin may have captured the essence of what we sought to do here when he wrote, "We can disagree and still love each other unless your disagreement is rooted in my oppression and denial of my humanity and right to exist."[1] In an era where denigrating and disavowing those who think differently is in vogue, we've tried to offer an alternative model, one for those who desire to disagree with grace and explore differences without rancor.

We finished this collaboration more confident than ever that we can acknowledge competing arguments without compromising our integrity or forsaking our beliefs. For those of us who choose to work in education, where we have taken upon ourselves the work of preparing the rising generation for life, liberty, and the pursuit of happiness, that must be the bar.

CHAPTER 1

Introduction

As is true of so much in our polarized age, our discussions about school-ing are riven by deep divides. In most any educational gathering today, one need only mention school choice, testing, or discipline for feathers to fly.

Once upon a time, education felt less rancorous and, well, less par-tisan. Twenty or 30 years ago, there were still sharp disagreements over many of these issues, but the debates were more measured.

That's no longer the case.

The two of us firmly believe that honest, principled debate can be a powerful force for good. But much of what's unfolding today feels less honest than angry and less principled than reflexively political. There's just not much room for good-faith disagreement.

It's easy for even the most measured disagreements to harden into distrust and disdain when the most common avenues for en-countering those with whom we disagree are angry Facebook posts or snarky tweets. Indeed, you might think that every dispute over school choice, testing, or discipline is a tussle between the kindly champions of justice and the agents of iniquity if you follow education debates on social media or cable news (which side is which depends on your source).

Part of what's going on is something that social scientists call "group polarization." As Cass Sunstein observed back in 1999, delib-eration among a group of like-minded individuals tends to make the whole group's views *more* extreme.[1] In other words, talking with those who think like we do doesn't open our minds; it intensifies and calci-fies our views. Groups can become so doctrinaire that simply having doubts or asking questions is seen as blasphemous. That's why con-versing with allies provides little insight into the thinking of those who disagree with us.

Meanwhile, the loudest and most extreme voices tend to get the most attention. Funders stand ready to support those who energetically push their agenda. Advocates celebrate and fete those who most stridently make their case. And, of course, there are media outlets looking to generate controversy in pursuit of clicks. This has all thrown gas on the raging fire of polarization.

The resulting conflagration has obscured the fact that many of our disagreements in education aren't as big as they can seem. On closer inspection, these bitter disputes are frequently rooted in honest, potentially reconcilable differences. Unfortunately, in education as in the nation, we have too few models for navigating these divides.

Universities and their schools of education, which we might expect to cultivate these exchanges, have not done much to bring together the competing sides in these debates. When conferences or convenings opt to feature a range of perspectives, the result is typically a public rehashing of disagreements rather than an attempt to traverse them. There's plenty of dogmatic punditry, but little that acknowledges complexity or illuminates difficult trade-offs.

There are, of course, efforts to seek common ground. Often, these entail blue-ribbon, bipartisan commissions issuing consensus documents on subjects like civics or social-emotional learning. The reports offer solemn prose, bury the disagreements under jargon, and close with some well-meaning action items. We've sat on our share of these commissions and think that, although they have value, they don't do much to promote deep understanding of disagreements.

In this book, we're seeking to do something different. We aren't trying to settle on a salable agenda or dazzle each other with esoteric data points. Instead, we're hoping to better understand where and why we disagree on some of the biggest education questions of our time. With this in mind, we seek to break free from the tyranny of pleasant phrases meant to paper over disagreements and instead try to expose our differences and lay our views out in the open. The format of this book—a series of back-and-forth exchanges that range over the most contentious issues in schooling—is intended to foster an actual conversation rather than a series of sound bites.

WHO WE ARE

Of course, this exercise will be a lot more interesting if you actually know who we are and how we come at these issues.

For readers who may not be familiar with Pedro, he was born in New York City, raised in Brooklyn and Queens, and attended high school in Brentwood, Long Island. The son of Caribbean immigrants, he attended Brown University, where he studied sociology and American history, earned a teaching credential, and participated in the antiapartheid movement. After Brown, Pedro taught social studies in Providence, Rhode Island, before going on to pursue his PhD in sociology at UC Berkeley. At Berkeley, Pedro served as president of the student body, executive assistant to the mayor of Berkeley, and on the Berkeley school board.

Pedro has been a professor at UC Berkeley, Harvard, NYU, and UCLA, and is now the dean of the Rossier School of Education at the University of Southern California. He's written hundreds of research articles and reports, and authored widely read books, including *City Schools and the American Dream, Creating the Opportunity to Learn* with A. Wade Boykin, and *The Trouble with Black Boys . . . and Other Reflections on Race, Equity, and the Future of Public Education.* A member of the National Academy of Education and the American Academy of Arts and Sciences, he's on the boards of *The Nation* magazine, the National Equity Project, and City Year Los Angeles and has received a number of awards and honorary doctorates for his work combating poverty and in urban education.

And for those who don't know Rick, he was born in Allentown, Pennsylvania, and spent his elementary school years getting beat up in New Jersey and northern Virginia. He subbed for pizza money while in college at Brandeis University, loved it, went on to earn his master's in education and teaching credential at Harvard University, and then taught high school social studies in Baton Rouge, Louisiana. There, as he recounts in *Letters to a Young Education Reformer,* he was mugged by the frustrations of school life. He returned to Harvard to pursue a PhD and make sense of what he'd seen. After earning his doctorate, he became a professor of education at the University of Virginia.

In 2002, Rick left UVA to launch the education policy program at the American Enterprise Institute, perhaps the nation's preeminent conservative think tank. Over the years, he's taught a bit at Harvard, the University of Pennsylvania, Rice, Georgetown, and Johns Hopkins. He pens the Rick Hess Straight Up blog for *Education Week* and serves as a senior contributor at *Forbes,* a contributor to *The Hill,* an executive editor of *Education Next,* and a board member for 4.0 Schools and the National Association of Charter School Authorizers. His books include *Cage-Busting Leadership, The Same Thing Over and Over, Common Sense School Reform,* and *Spinning Wheels.* Unlike Pedro, he's garnered no awards or honorary degrees. (So it goes.)

It's fair to say that we've disagreed a fair bit over the past couple decades, with Pedro generally on the Left and Rick mostly on the Right. When it comes to school choice, for instance, Pedro once told the *Wall Street Journal* that he left his position on the State University of New York Board of Trustees in part because he saw "a deliberate attempt to create competition between public and charter schools."[2] Rick, on the other hand, explained in a *Harvard Ed. Magazine* profile that he's all for "consequential competition" in education, so long as there are appropriate guardrails.[3]

Pedro and Rick have both taken to the pages of the *New York Times* to write about the Common Core standards for math and English language arts, with Pedro encouraging their adoption and Rick arguing that this kind of one-size-fits-all reform tends to fall flat.[4] On school funding, Pedro has argued in the *Washington Post* that there's a need to "restore funding for education equity," while Rick has warned against unqualified demands for more money, arguing in *U.S. News & World Report* that such demands too often overshadow attention to "how dollars are being spent."[5] And, on teacher tenure, Rick has written in *USA Today* that tenure should be curtailed, whereas Pedro has defended it, countering that tenure is essential if low-income schools are to attract and keep good teachers.[6]

Indeed, one could probably make a (very boring) parlor game of perusing our books, essays, and op-eds to find all the places we've disagreed over the course of many years. Given this, we didn't expect to discover that we secretly agreed on lots of big questions. But we were curious to see where we did agree and how much common ground we'd unearth.

FINDING A WAY FORWARD, TOGETHER

We spoke a moment ago about "group polarization." Well, as a nation, we've come to a point where it's so severe that millions of overwrought Americans say they hate those who inhabit the other end of the political spectrum.[7] Horrifically, 20% of Democrats and 16% of Republicans said in 2019 that they sometimes think, "We'd be better off as a country if large numbers of the opposing party in the public today just died."

But these depressing results also suggest that 80% or more of Americans are capable of recognizing that there are decent people on the other side of our ideological divides. A big problem is that our public debates have been hijacked by a subset of unyielding, unhinged true believers.

In 2019, the nonprofit More in Common examined the enormous "perception gap" in the United States.[8] The bottom line? Those most engaged in politics have the most distorted perceptions of those on the other side. Watching more cable news or reading more about politics on social media made respondents *less* informed about the actual views of their political opponents. It's bizarre: Progressive and conservative activists alike were sure that their opponents were more extreme than they actually were.

In fact, an overwhelming majority of Americans say that "compromise and common ground should be the goal for political leaders," even as they add that they are "tired of leaders compromising my values and ideals."[9] In short, it seems to us that Americans are tired both of hyperbolic politics and of leaders who fail to stand up for their values.

The challenge is to square that circle: to fight for the things we believe in, but in a manner that respects our opponents, identifies common ground, and points the way to principled cooperation. This is a universal challenge. But it may be especially pressing in education, where our charge includes forming citizens, imparting our shared values, and ensuring that equal opportunity is a sacred promise and not a hollow hope.

This book is our attempt to do better on that score, in a manner that might encourage similar conversations in schools and communities. In this effort, we've drawn inspiration from the years-long correspondence between John Adams and Thomas Jefferson, our second and third presidents. Founders of the two great political parties of their era, they fought furiously about foreign policy, commerce, faith, slavery, and much else. Yet they also engaged in an intimate correspondence that spanned decades. When they resumed their exchange at one point, after a dozen years of silence, Adams wistfully wrote, "You and I ought not to die, before we have explained ourselves to each other."[10] A worthy goal, indeed.

ABOUT THIS BOOK

More than anything else, our aim in this book is to light a candle, one illuminating that it's possible to hash out tough questions and find points of common ground even on the thorniest issues.

So, who should read this book?

We've written it for superintendents and school leaders who seek a model for more fully engaging their communities and staffs; for professors and teacher educators who talk about the importance of empathy and courageous conversation but have too few models on which to draw; and for school boards and public officials who want to better understand competing views on heated issues like testing, school choice, or diversity.

We've written for teachers who want to more fully make sense of the debates that suffuse their profession, and for advocates and foundation staff seeking a window into the disputes they're asked to navigate on a daily basis.

We've written this for those who understand that civil debate and principled disagreement are essential to a thriving democracy. And we've written for those who appreciate that the future of this remarkable land will turn in large measure by what happens in our schools.

What can readers expect to find in the pages ahead?

The chapters consist of a series of back-and-forth conversations addressing hot-button debates over testing, school choice, and privatization; pressing concerns like social–emotional learning, philanthropy, and teacher pay; and sensitive questions around the purpose of schooling, civics education, and diversity and equity.

The correspondence played out as a continuous series of emails between January and July 2020. Sometimes the conversation flowed easily; sometimes it was more difficult. The exchanges were, by turns, personal and philosophical, raw and reflective, evidence-laced and emotionally charged. We hope that readers learn even half as much from perusing these pages as we did from penning them.

While we were in the midst of this effort, the United States was suddenly struck by the novel coronavirus, causing a surreal national shutdown—including the sudden closure of 100,000 schools across the land. And then, less than two months later, the nation was swept by protests and urban unrest on a scale not seen in a half century. The police killing of George Floyd in Minneapolis triggered a national outcry over racial justice, one that quickly took center stage in conversations about schooling.

This book is not about those events; it's about education more broadly. But they were the backdrop on which we were writing and served as reminders of just how central a role schooling plays in our lives. Families were looking to schools for meals, social–emotional support, and remote instruction, and the education conversation was suffused with discussion of policing, systemic bias, and how to help students negotiate the role of race in American life.

We've each spent decades in and around education—in classrooms, schools, board meetings, green rooms, conferences, secretive consultations, and the halls of power. And, through it all, we've both been troubled that goodwill and good sense can get lost amid all the shouting.

When we disagree with someone, it can be easy to assume that our differences are the result of their ignorance or malice. Although that may occasionally be the case, we've found over the years that it's generally not. Often, these disagreements are simply products of different experiences, perspectives, and views. Understanding those can alter our thinking and our judgments.

Opening ourselves up to other perspectives does not mean we're abandoning our own convictions, only that we believe in hearing people out before deciding we've nothing to learn from them. And, really, it's hard to imagine educators operating in accord with any other principle. With that, let's get started.

CHAPTER 2

The Purpose of Schooling

Rick and Pedro kick off their correspondence with a question that sits at the core of any conversation about education: What is the purpose of schooling? Our authors ultimately agree that education has twin purposes, the academic and the social. When it comes to the academic mission, the goals are relatively straightforward: to pass on knowledge and prepare students to generate new ideas and knowledge throughout their lifetimes. When it comes to the social purpose, though, things are less clear. Pedro fears that it's possible to get so caught up in idealistic debates about the social mission that we fail to wrestle with what it actually takes for schools to model the values we want kids to learn. Rick argues that, whatever the practical challenges, the social aspect is "vital for successful schools." In the end, finding agreement on purpose was easier than our authors anticipated, perhaps, Rick postulates, because broad notions of mission matter less than the particulars of how that mission is brought to life. Key issues include how to define the purpose of education, balance the academic and social missions of education, and navigate concerns implied by the social mission.

Dear Rick,

I'm looking forward to our exchange. I'm hoping it can serve as an opportunity for us to communicate about some of the controversies and conflicts that have characterized, and at times paralyzed, the field of education. You and I have known each other for several years, and while we often disagree about many of these issues, we have also shown that we can do so respectfully. I think lots of people could benefit from seeing us model a healthy, civil exchange of ideas.

To get us started, I'd like to pose some questions about education itself. The pandemic has given me lots of time to ponder the purpose of school, particularly because I'm hearing so many parents complain about online schooling and watching my own daughter become increasingly disgruntled and unmotivated. The current situation has made me wonder what we're trying to accomplish.

So first, I think it's helpful to consider the functions of schooling—what schools actually do—and then use that as a springboard to think about schools' purpose. I see schooling as having three primary functions: social, economic, and political.

First, schools are critical to socialization and citizenship. We rely on them to teach kids to understand our rules and customs, and to function as members of society. In school, kids learn about the meaning of race, gender, sexuality, and lots of other things that help to maintain the social order. In many cases, these lessons are delivered implicitly through subtle socialization processes.

This kind of socialization isn't always for the better. To illustrate this point, I often ask how many of my university students know what the cooties are, and all of the U.S.-born students raise their hands. When I ask them to explain the concept to students who were not born in the United States, they explain that cooties are used to keep boys and girls apart. When we probe further, it becomes clear that cooties are also used to ostracize kids who are different: too fat, too slow, too dark, too different. The interesting thing about cooties is that the game is typically not taught by teachers but by other kids who pass it down from generation to generation across the country. It's remarkable when you think about it. I think it speaks to the powerful way in which our schools perpetuate social norms and ostracize those who don't conform.

Second, schools have an economic function. We count on schools to sort out our division of labor—who will do which job. While some kids are being actively prepared for managerial and professional roles, others are prepared for menial labor. We don't explicitly tell the kids who end up in blue-collar jobs where they're heading, but everything else, from the curriculum to the formal and informal messages they receive about their future, does. This is one of the reasons why kids from working-class backgrounds are more likely to end up in the military while kids from affluent families almost never do, and why so many low-income kids of color get stuck permanently in low-wage jobs.[1] Too often, our schools are largely reproducing inequality and privilege across generations.

Finally, our schools are inherently political. In fact, they are part of the state, the administrative apparatus of government, like highways, airports, and the health care system. As we see clearly now during the pandemic, schools are essential for the functioning of a modern society. The economy can't reopen until schools do, and many children rely on schools for meals.

The political function of schools involves more than just supervising kids. It reminds us that schools are also where children learn American values like patriotism. This is more than citizenship, which could be thought of as ideologically neutral. Schools promote political loyalty through rituals like the pledge of allegiance, the holidays we celebrate, and the way they teach social studies. The big problem is that this often results in a tendency to gloss over or completely ignore negative aspects of American history (e.g., slavery, genocide, segregation, etc.), as well an unwillingness to critically probe our domestic and foreign policy. When your goal is to produce loyal citizens, critical thinking usually loses out.

Now, because what I've described here are really the functions of school, they don't get at the purpose. Forgive me for getting too academic here, but the function of something is about how it's used, not why it exists. The why, or purpose, in my opinion, is linked to two contradictory goals.

First, we count on schools to pass on the knowledge accumulated by previous generations to the next generation. This way kids don't have to relearn how to do things we already figured out in the past, like how to make fire, use a wheel, or produce penicillin.

Second, we also count on schools and education generally to produce new ideas and new knowledge—which requires that kids be grounded in empathy, integrity, compassion, and cooperation. Without this, it will be impossible to achieve progress in the future because the knowledge and values (competition, individualism, racism, etc.) that have been taught in the past have left us with the problems of the present. We need new ideas and technology to tackle diseases and climate change, and we need new knowledge and a more widespread embrace of humanitarian values to figure out how to solve problems that previous generations couldn't solve, like poverty, war, and inequality.

Both of these purposes are important, but, in my opinion, kids in school are much more likely to be prepared with the first goal (passing along accumulated knowledge) in mind than the second (producing new ideas). I believe we must actively pursue both: Kids need the ability to function in society as it is, but they also need to be armed with the critical thinking, creativity, and problem-solving ability to change society for the better.

How do we ensure that there is a balance in the pursuit of both goals?

I look forward to hearing back from you, my friend.–Pedro

Dear Pedro,

I'm looking forward to this little journey of ours. We've both had our fill of speechifying and social media squabbling. I'm curious to see if we can do better, learn a bit from each other, and perhaps find some common ground. Thanks for so thoughtfully launching us on our way.

You point to transmitting knowledge and producing new knowledge as the two purposes of schooling. With your permission, I'll make a small (but significant) modification to your second goal. It seems to me that our aim in K–12 is less about producing new knowledge than equipping students to *eventually* do so. When it comes to higher education, the calculus is obviously different. If you're comfortable with that modification, then I heartily embrace your goals.

But, and here's the crucial "but," I think those goals only capture half of schooling's purpose. For me, the twin purposes of schooling are academic and social. You've clearly sketched out the academic mission in your letter, but it's more nebulous whether you think there's a complementary social mission. That may or may not be a meaningful point of disagreement. Let me say a bit more and then we'll see.

We are social creatures. Kids need schools not just to learn or to learn how to learn, but to find mentors, make friends, interact with a mix of people, explore new roles, cultivate empathy and self-discipline, and see our shared values in practice. Over the decades, as civil society has atrophied, schools have been asked to take on more and more of this burden, playing a role once shouldered more widely by institutions like churches, Scout troops, and 4-H clubs.

It's hardly a new notion, of course, to suggest that schools should teach civic and social skills. Indeed, the architects of American education–thinkers like Benjamin Rush and Horace Mann–unapologetically believed that indoctrination in the civic virtues was at the core of public education. The aim was to teach students the habits of mind that would equip them to be good citizens—or "republican machines," in Rush's infelicitous phrase.[2]

For me, this charge is central to the mission of schooling, even if I think schools get some of it wrong and if we're inevitably going to disagree about just how to define those virtues.

Yet I appreciate that the intellectual and social missions of schooling can conflict when this civic dimension is elevated. The push to cultivate desired habits of mind, for instance, can clash with efforts to cultivate free thinkers. Thus, any conversation about the purpose of education is, in part, about how to reconcile the tensions.

To be clear, none of this should be read as an attempt to waffle on schooling's academic charge. Schools are the places where youth learn the knowledge, skills, and habits needed to be responsible, autonomous citizens. This is schooling's distinctive responsibility. In almost any community, there are many adults—from cousins to coaches—who may be able to mentor a child, teach social skills, or provide a shoulder to cry on. Few, aside from educators, are prepared to coherently teach algebra, biology, or Spanish. So the academic piece must be inviolate.

It's no wonder emotions can run so hot when we argue about how well schools are doing. If there are competing purposes, as I suggest, it means two people can view a school and come to very different judgments about how well it's doing, making it all too easy for us to talk past one another. How do you think about this whole question of the social mission, my friend?

Best,
Rick

Dear Rick,

Let's talk about academic purpose first, then I'll circle back to your thoughts on socialization.

I like the way you modified my point about schools preparing kids to produce new knowledge. I overstated the point in my last letter, but I think we agree that if kids are involved in learning activities that encourage critical thinking, problem solving, and creativity, they are more likely to contribute to the production of new knowledge in the future. So, it seems we agree that when it comes to academic mission, schools should both pass on accumulated knowledge and prepare kids to discover more.

My concern is that schools are far more focused on the first academic objective–passing along accumulated knowledge so kids are prepared for society as it is–at the expense of the second–preparing kids to acquire skills like problem solving and critical thinking so that they can play a role in changing and improving society. Kids deserve more, and our society certainly needs more from its schools.

If we recognized the value of having kids experience joy in learning, we might have an easier time balancing the two academic missions. I'm from a working-class background, and before I left for college, my father, who had not graduated from high school, said this: "You can get a free education with a library card." He was speaking from experience because he was an avid reader, especially books on history and geography, his two favorite subjects. However, he added this: "Don't go to college and study something you could have learned for free at the library." [period] When he found out that I was going to major in sociology and history, he told me I could have definitely learned that in the library. His concern was that with a social science major, I wouldn't find a job.

What my father didn't see is that I had a passion for history and sociology. Math and science were not my forte, so if I had chosen a path that led to medicine (what he would have preferred), not only would I have struggled academically, I also wouldn't have enjoyed it very much. Fortunately, by studying what I loved, I not only found a job but a guiding passion.

This raises the question: Where does the joy of learning fit into the academic purpose of schools? I know that not every aspect of learning will be joyful. I did well in geometry and physics while in high school, but the only joy I experienced in those subjects was seeing the courses end. By learning to overcome my fear of those subjects and struggling through the parts that were difficult for me, I gained a feeling of accomplishment. As Aristotle reminds us: "The roots of education are bitter, but the fruit is sweet."[3] Learning to work through difficult subjects should be part of the academic experience, too.

You spoke at length about the socialization that occurs in school, and although I think that is an important part of school, I have a different perspective on how it plays out. I recently saw a poll that about 10% of kids have reported enjoying distance learning more than traditional school.[4] Many of these kids report that they enjoy learning at their own pace, not being overwhelmed with pressure from taking too many rigorous courses, and no longer being hassled or bullied by peers. Prior to the pandemic, we were seeing large numbers of kids, many of them high achievers, who were suffering from depression and anxiety. I imagine that school doesn't bring much joy to many of these kids.

The truth is: A lot of kids go to school in spite of—not because of—the social experience. Bullying and racist harassment were a regular part of my school experience. I had to learn how to deal with bullies, how to defend myself when threatened, and how to stand up for myself when teachers or other kids attempted to put me down because of my race. I know there's more to socialization than this, but if the educators are not attentive to how students treat one another, and if they are not intentional about teaching empathy, kindness, honesty, and integrity, school can be a rough place for lots of kids.

So, what do we do to ensure that the socialization kids experience in school helps them to grow in positive ways and nurtures the type of character traits we both agree are important?—Pedro

---

Dear Pedro,

I found myself chuckling as I read your dad's advice. Sounds like my kind of guy—sharp and with a healthy dose of skepticism. "You can get a free education with a library card." He was right, of course. And yet I think there's more to the story. I want to stay with that for a moment because it goes to the heart of this discussion.

Your dad's words reminded me of the Obama-era love affair with massive open online courses (MOOCs), which are basically a high-tech version of that free library education. I can still recall *The Atlantic* declaring that these free online courses, open to anyone with an Internet connection, were unleashing a "revolution" in higher education.[5] Popularized by world-renowned professors at places like Stanford and MIT, some attracted tens of thousands of registrants.

But the revolution stalled out pretty quickly. Even though students were adult learners taking the classes voluntarily, the overwhelming majority didn't actually complete them. Fewer than one out of 20 enrollees completed a typical MOOC class at Harvard or MIT.[6] These offerings worked for a smattering of students but not for most.

I think MOOCs didn't live up to the hype because they were missing essential elements of what good schooling entails. After all, there's a lot that an education acquired via a library card doesn't include because there's a lot of connective tissue that's missing when you wander into a library and pull books off the shelf. When you do that, you don't have someone to provide context, offer structure and sequence, help you through the confusing parts, answer questions, talk through implications, put a hand on your shoulder during the rough patches, or gauge when you've mastered what matters.

Schools can provide that human interaction and direction that makes learning more than a matter of pages or pixels. Now, not every single one of us needs the human dimension. There are certainly self-taught savants. And there are surely times and subjects when the human touch may matter less. But most of the time, for most of us, mentoring, support, and connection make a big difference in our ability to learn and grow as people and citizens. This is why I put so much stock in that social dimension.

Good schools augment and amplify what a solitary learner can glean in the library. And yet as you note, schools too often fall woefully short on the social mission. I recognize this reality but don't regard this failure as an argument against the principle. Indeed, the traumas you so movingly describe are powerful evidence that schools will inevitably be in the business of modeling and teaching values and that it's therefore vital they pursue this work wisely and well.

It's in this context that I consider your wonderful query regarding the role of joy in learning. My off-the-cuff answer is that the joy of learning should loom large. That said, I think education—like any worthy endeavor—should entail both joy and struggle. Whether we're talking about sports, playing a musical instrument, or video gaming, mastery is always a process that involves both tears and triumph. Any accomplished athlete, musician, litigator, physician, or mathematician can talk at length about the rigor and tedium that excellence demands—and also about the joy of discovery, of putting their gifts to work, of losing themselves in the act.

That applies to pretty much all real learning, I suspect, whatever the skill or subject. That's why schools should be places of both challenge and joy.

Look, I totally get your description of the fear you felt as a student. I'm with you. In elementary school, I was beaten up and bullied on a regular basis—just getting on the school bus was a fear-inducing exercise. In high school, I was flatly terrified of my classes in French and science, given my knack for finding awkward new ways to reveal my ignorance. Fear sucks. We agree.

Even so, I believe there's a healthy role for a certain kind of "fear." There's something innately anxiety-inducing about doing something we haven't yet mastered—whether that's riding a bike or delivering a speech. I find that the first steps toward mastery are always accompanied by a fear of failure or embarrassment. Learning is a process of conquering those fears.

I've always understood that great surgeons, scholars, and skate-boarders are fueled, in part, by a fear of failure—that this provides an internal discipline that helps fuel their drive to excel. I know that every time I write, I fear penning something foolish. Over the years, this fear has certainly prodded me to work harder than I otherwise might.

Again, don't get me wrong. I don't mean to endorse fear per se, especially not when it involves bullying, mockery, or hostile remarks. But I do think that fear is an organic part of learning—and that whether it's healthy or harmful is largely a question of coaching and context.

We agree that too few schools are equal to our aspirations. How can being more thoughtful about purpose help us start to change that?

Best,

Rick

Rick,

I agree that socialization is an important part of teaching students the joy and struggles of learning, and I didn't mean to imply otherwise, but I worry that you focus too much on the idealistic side of school purpose and so ignore the practical side of this debate. After all, you can argue all day that schools, in theory, should support socialization. The problem is that many don't do this, as I know from visiting hundreds of schools over the years.

So, let's talk about how to bridge the gap between what is and what should be. I've seen enough schools to know that it's possible. The question is: How do we help more schools to at least strive to create this kind of climate/culture?

Well, cultures can't be imposed on schools. We can't mandate kindness or respectful relationships any more than we can require people in society to live together in peace. Laws can at least minimize harm, but as we can see from crime data, mass shootings, and the high level of everyday violence, even our laws have limited ability to keep us safe.

As is true in society, we don't want schools to have to rely on rules to achieve a degree of safety and order. Ideally, these should be by-products of healthy relationships. How do we nurture healthy relation-ships? Again, I've been to schools where this is the norm.

A few years ago I visited a school in Queens, New York. It was a charter school, one of the few where all of the staff are in unions. Like many New York schools, it was tall, and each floor (it had 13) was dedicated to a specific grade: First floor was kindergarten, but the space featured a large play structure that the classrooms shared. Another floor was for 4th-graders, and the shared space had a stage. The seniors occupied the top floor and it featured a greenhouse where kids planted vegetables. I was so impressed by the thoughtfulness that went into the space, and I could tell it reflected the kind of caring cul-ture we've been talking about.

At one point we ran into a student wearing a baseball hat, and I asked the assistant principal who was giving me the tour if they al-lowed kids to wear hats at school. He called the student over and asked him to explain why he was wearing his hat. The student rolled his eyes as if this was going to take too much of his precious time, then reluc-tantly explained that a group of Muslim girls had petitioned the school for the right to wear headscarves because it was how they honored their culture and religion. The matter was discussed at a town meeting and they voted to allow Muslim girls to wear headscarves.

The following week, a group of Sikh boys petitioned for the right to wear turbans, which is also a requirement of their religion and culture. Once again, the school used a town hall meeting of students and staff to discuss the matter, and they voted to allow the Sikh boys to wear turbans. The following week, a group of kids petitioned to wear base-ball hats; they claimed that it was part of hip-hop culture and should be allowed. At the town hall meeting there was an impasse: Teachers refused to go along with allowing baseball hats in school. To resolve the matter, a subcommittee of students was created to try to work out a compromise. A week later the subcommittee proposed that kids could earn the right to wear a hat but only in the hallways, only if they had perfect attendance for the month, and only if they had a B average or better. The student explained that when you see a student wearing a hat, it's a sign of accomplishment, and they never fight over hats anymore.

This may seem like a trivial example, but how many schools have you visited where kids are constantly getting into trouble for hats, headphones, cell phones, and so forth? How often have you visited a school where kids are being actively prepared to participate in our democracy by experiencing democratic practice in their schools? This is just one of many examples I could cite of schools that have figured out how to make sure that the socialization they offer is aligned with the values they affirm.

Visiting schools like this one reminds me that schools can be places where kids can experience the joys and struggles that come with education, and where they can also learn to be part of a community and the responsibility that entails.—Pedro

---

Dear Pedro,

You're right that we can't mandate kindness or respect. Indeed, these terms—and talk of "socialization" more generally—can hit our ears in very different ways, depending on our own experiences. And yet I think we agree that values like kindness and respect are vital for successful schools and necessary if we're to help students grow into responsible adults.

That's why I want to be sure to take a moment to stay with your conversation in Queens. I think the anecdote resonated so strongly with me because it illustrates how we can get unstuck. As I read your tale, I saw an empowered student invested in the culture around him. I saw a school unapologetically socializing students in responsible ways while giving them agency and ownership.

In your depiction, I saw participatory democracy, personal responsibility, a culture of kindness, and a healthy respect for difference. In short, I saw a school engaged in both the intellectual and social dimensions of schooling. The trick, of course, is translating that culture from a single campus to whole systems of schools. That's where we have struggled, time and again.

It strikes me that there are at least three giant challenges when we try to translate high-minded talk of purpose into practice: deciding what schools should teach, figuring out what this means in practice, and then changing what schools actually do.

Oddly enough, this exchange has me thinking that a conversation I might've expected to be contentious—namely, "What should schools teach?"—turned out to be remarkably tractable. We seem to have settled pretty rapidly on the broad strokes.

I suppose, in retrospect, I shouldn't be so surprised. When working with school board members or school leaders, the big challenge is rarely getting them to agree on a list of stuff they want schools to teach (whether that's a matter of content, character, or something else).

More difficult is reaching agreement on what this stuff translates to in practice. Does "respect" mean taking a hat off when entering a classroom? Does it mean demanding a great deal from students, or does it mean letting students decide how much work they can handle? Does it mean addressing adults in a certain way? On all of this, there's a lot of disagreement rooted in our views, values, and experiences.

Harder still than agreeing on aspirations is getting schools to actually change in ways that reflect these aims. Most of the time, such attempts get squelched by disagreement, routines, and inertia.

For all that, we seem to have wound up broadly aligned on the purpose of schooling. We both embrace the academic mission, and I think we agree on the social mission—though the observation that schools tend not to do it well raises the question about whether we should trust them to tackle it.

In an era as polarized and frustrated as ours, disagreements can rage out of control. They can blot out everything else, obscuring points of commonality and the chance for mutual understanding. This exchange has reminded me of how vital and possible it is for people of goodwill to push back. With that, I'm looking forward to wading into some of those particulars.

Be well, my friend.

Best,

Rick

CHAPTER 3

School Choice

School choice is among the most contentious topics in education. The debate often devolves into a shouting match between supporters railing against "failing government schools" and opponents decrying a mean-spirited attack on public education. Rick and Pedro eschew the familiar talking points, opting for a more substantive and amiable tenor as they set out on a wide-ranging meditation on the promise and perils of choice. Rick supports choice because he believes it offers a path to "organic, personal" school improvement, contending that it has the power to "liberate families and educators from the familiar bureaucratic apparatus" while making it easier to serve students and families with diverse needs. The allure of school choice, he says, is not a mechanistic promise of higher test scores but its ability to empower marginalized families, foster opportunities for reinvention, and allow more coherent, mission-driven school communities. Pedro, on the other hand, remains skeptical, observing that choice has too often been sold as a panacea, distracting from—and sometimes exacerbating—the real problems that plague America's schools. He fears that choice allows schools to pick their students, aggravating existing inequities. Critical questions in this chapter include how to make the case for and against school choice and whether there are places where the two sides can find principled compromise.

Dear Pedro,

When it comes to school choice, it's easy to fall into familiar, dead-end arguments that offer more heat than light. Here's hoping our exchange will be a little more illuminating.

I'll start by being clear about where I stand: I broadly support school choice, including vouchers, charter schools, educational savings accounts, home schooling, and the rest. I support choice, even though I think the evidence on testing outcomes is far from dispositive and depends on the program in question. And I support choice, even while conceding that there can be much to like about traditional public school districts.

So, I'm not arguing that school choice is a cure-all or that traditional district schools are "failing." Given that, why *do* I support it?

Well, for a number of reasons. I think all parents have a right to seek a safe, responsive learning environment for their child, whether or not they have resources. Given that education inevitably traffics in deeply personal questions of morality and conduct, I believe that, generally speaking, parents deserve the opportunity to send their kids to schools that respect their values and their faith. When families exercise choice, parents are more satisfied with their schools, students feel safer, and the effects on things like graduation and achievement tend to be neutral or positive.[1] And given that children have very different needs, more diverse options better enable parents to find schools and programs that are a good fit for their child.

But, for me, the most compelling argument may be that choice can foster organic, personal school improvement. Now, admittedly, people tend to look at me sideways when I talk this way. That's not how advocates usually champion school choice. More often, they make a mechanistic case: School choice lifts reading and math scores and therefore "works." But I think that such talking points ignore the complicated reality and undersell the promise of choice.

Choice can liberate families and educators from the familiar bureaucratic apparatus. Rather than asking every school to be a one-stop shop for every child in an attendance zone, choice allows new schools to emerge, founders to forge coherent school communities, educators to more easily find schools that reflect their own pedagogy and practice, and parents to choose the schools that work for their child. This all constitutes an appealing alternative to "reform," which relies on political combat and a succession of mass-produced, rigid directives.

I've had far too many conversations over the decades with teachers, principals, and district leaders who pepper their thoughts with phrases like, "I'd like to do this but the contract requires," or "I'd love to use this program but they tell me I can't do it with those funds because . . ." Even when formally empowered to act, school and system leaders are hamstrung by ingrained customs and culture.

In any sector, organizations tend to grow rigid with time. They run into trouble as their needs change. This is as true of companies, nonprofits, and government agencies as it is of school systems. After all, an organization's culture embodies certain assumptions about pay, routines, job descriptions, staffing, work schedules, and more. As the world evolves, it's remarkably tough to rethink all of this, summon the will to pursue sweeping changes, or convince longtime employees to get on board. It's really difficult to say, "Guess what, everyone? We're starting from scratch!"

To be fair, it's not like districts never change. They change all the time. But the changes tend to be inch deep, precisely because anything more can be painful, politically perilous, and dependent on altering deeply rooted rules, contracts, and routines. Before they ever get going, educators seeking deep changes exhaust themselves just battling for permission to act. As a result, people tinker, persuade themselves this tinkering is more significant than it is, and hope that'll do the trick.

School choice makes it much easier to start new schools with the kind of clear mission, shared expectations, and faculty and parental buy-in that's crucial to any school's success. New schools of choice can adopt the instructional programs, calendars, and staffing models that suit without having to unwind what's already in place or negotiate with obdurate stakeholders.

Anyway, although I know that's not how many of my friends make the case, that's how I see things. Where do you stand on the school choice question, my friend?

Best,

Rick

Dear Rick,

I'm ready to tackle choice with you and to do it in ways that I hope will shed more light than confusion. Merely rehashing old debates is not likely to generate much in the way of new understanding or help us in carving out a fair and reasonable path forward.

I will say at the outset where we are in disagreement: I don't support vouchers or for-profit charter schools. In my opinion, both lead to profiteering and open the door to the exploitation of parents and kids as we've seen in Detroit. When the state took control of Detroit's schools in 1999, rather than reinvesting and ushering in an era of improvement, the state imposed choice and charters as its remedy for the failing district. Over a 10-year period, over 40% of the charter schools in Detroit closed.[2] Instead of increasing access to better schools, the proliferation of charter schools contributed to more parents fleeing a weakened school system.

Detroit is not the only city that experienced this type of decline during the heyday of choice. Baltimore, Philadelphia, Chicago, Washington, D.C., and others also experienced mass school closures without the benefit of large-scale improvement. My question to you is: When it is clear that choice has not improved access to or the availability of good schools, how much choice do parents really have?

Rick, you said that "all parents have a right to seek a safe, responsive learning environment for their child, whether or not they have resources." I say, there is no evidence that choice levels the playing field in any way that guarantees access for poor kids of color to go to better schools. Even if we concede that at least a third of charter schools are getting better test scores than comparable public schools, several studies have shown that charter schools are more likely to under-enroll the kids with the greatest needs, such as English learners, homeless students, or children in foster care.[3] When charter schools are able to avoid responsibility for educating the neediest kids, it increases the concentration of these kids in public schools.

Having stated that, I must also say that I'm not entirely opposed to nonprofit charter schools, especially those that have been organized at the grassroots, community level by parents and educators.

To provide an example of when I am open to supporting charter schools: I recently signed a petition to support one in Los Angeles County because I learned that the school was being designed specifically to serve children who are homeless, in foster care, or whose parents are incarcerated. The proposal called for housing to be provided to these children and for the school to offer a broad array of social services. After I signed the petition, I was contacted by the superintendent of the district where the school will be located and asked why I would support a charter school coming into his district. I simply pointed out that his district had such a poor track record in serving the kinds of kids this school was being created for, I felt it was worth trying something new. I also told him that if he was serious about trying to keep children from enrolling in the charter school, he should devise a convincing plan for serving these vulnerable kids, otherwise it will look like he just wanted them to maintain his school's enrollment. I haven't heard back from him again.

I have found that there is lots of hypocrisy in the debate over choice and charter schools. Many of the people who oppose charter schools don't object to public schools that screen out disadvantaged kids or that fail to serve them well. For this reason, although it has frequently been difficult, I try to maintain a nuanced stance toward charter schools.

As you may know, I served as a charter school authorizer for the State University of New York (SUNY). For the three years I held the post, I was generally proud of what we accomplished. However, I very publicly resigned from my post as it became clear some of the charter schools we had authorized were being used to displace traditional public schools that were working well and serving very disadvantaged neighborhoods. In too many cases, the charter schools we authorized were good, but they had no commitment to the kids in the neighborhoods where the schools were located and in many cases were not serving the most vulnerable kids.

The last straw for me came when a charter school we authorized was allowed to displace a school for severely disabled children. The advocates for the charter school had board members from large banks like Goldman Sachs and private hedge funds. They came to our hearing with lawyers to make the case for them. In contrast, the only advocates for the school serving the severely disabled were a few parents and teachers.

This was not an isolated case. On several occasions, I saw charter management organizations funded by the well-heeled that had little regard for how other children were being impacted in the fight over precious real estate. In several cities, there is a limited supply of space for schools, so when a charter is created, it must either share space with an existing school or, in some cases, displace a school entirely. In Detroit, new charter schools enticed families with gifts like laptops and special field trips and electives like music that were not available to children in traditional public schools. Throughout the country, public schools are already characterized by extreme inequality in quality and the opportunities they provide to students. I believe that more often than not, choice makes inequality even worse.

However, I recognize that not all charter schools are the same, which is why I can't say that I am opposed to them. There's incredible diversity among charter schools, and some offer the kind of culturally responsive, community-engaged education that I admire. I know charter schools that are deeply committed to equity, to bilingual education, to project-based learning, and to performance-based assessment.

For this reason, when I discuss choice and charter schools, I try to make a distinction between the policy effects of choice and the rights of parents to find the best schools for their kids. All parents want what's best for their children, but often when schools make an effort to be the "best," it results in them pushing out kids with behavior problems or who struggle academically. I realize this may sound indecisive and conflicted, but this is a complicated situation: Not all charter schools do this, but some do, and they shouldn't be allowed to get away with it. Generalizing in this debate never helps, and when we don't acknowledge good opportunities being created for kids or kids being harmed by the worst offenders, it adds to the deepening of polarization.

I'll close here: It seems to me that choice never works as a way to ensure equity in educational opportunity unless there are many good choices available to all kinds of families. This doesn't mean all schools should be the same but rather that a baseline of quality must be maintained. Without this assurance, choice inevitably becomes a means of rationing access to the best schools. Who gets advantaged under a rationing system? Generally, it's the parents who have access to information, transportation, powerful connections, and so forth.

Choice is producing winners and losers, and when this is allowed, it's not only bad for the kids who lose but for society as a whole. Do you share this concern?—Pedro

---

Dear Pedro,

I'll begin with your closing question: Yep, I do think that educational choices create winners and losers. But I also think the same is true of systems that restrict choice, denying some families the power and options enjoyed by others. The difference is that I believe choice helps yield more good opportunities for everyone—especially the kids ill-served by a lack of choice.

I'll say more, but let me first acknowledge all of your concerns.

You're right that the charter school sector has its share of troubling behavior. Of course, the same is true of traditional districts—and I'm not at all confident which is worse.

You're right that there have been times when and places where facilities are at a premium, and it's tough to accommodate charters. I'd argue that this isn't the case in most places; more common, perhaps, is districts running half-full schools or sitting on underutilized buildings due to board politics and bureaucratic inertia.

You're right that some charter schools don't serve as many children with special needs. Now, part of this is a consequence of charters effectively serving in general education classrooms some students who might otherwise be flagged as special needs.[4] More broadly, though, many charters are successful precisely because they're small and mission centric—which can leave them less able to duplicate all the services a district can provide. (And plenty of district schools struggle with special education, too, of course, by overidentifying some groups or relying on outsourcing some hard-to-serve students to specialized private providers.)[5]

I can go on, but my takeaway wouldn't change. In each case, you raise legitimate concerns—but I find them far less troubling when I ask, "Compared to what?" You're right that people are making choices, and this has consequences. For me, the larger point is that humans will *always* make choices. When policy seeks to restrict these, parents will strive to make them by other means—whether that's leaning on a principal to move a student to a preferred teacher's classroom, or for those with resources, buying a home in a community with "better" schools.

Now, I'm *not* saying that "whatever problems charter schools have, traditional district schools are worse." What I am saying is that, whatever school choice's shortcomings, students and families are generally worse off without it. School choice has made possible the emergence of more good options, especially in poor and minority communities where kids are otherwise stuck in struggling schools. I'm thinking of schools like New York's 15,000-student Success Academy Charter Schools, which educate mostly low-income, minority students with extraordinary academic results (and lots of chess and poetry, for good measure). This is good for those kids, their families, and our sense of the possible.[6]

I fully appreciate that Success Academy isn't to everyone's liking. As Robert Pondiscio so compellingly argued in *How the Other Half Learns,* a big part of Success Academy's, well, success is that it sets rigorous expectations for students *and* their parents or guardians.[7] Some who see this culture as elitist regard it as a problem. I see it as a tribute to what schools of choice can accomplish.

After all, we agree that it can be incredibly tough for schools or systems to get all the oars pulling in the same direction. This isn't because people don't care or are malicious; it's because school systems include lots of people with different ideas on instruction, discipline, expectations, and everything else. That can make organizational or instructional coherence a pipe dream.

In my experience, great schools are cocreated; they depend on students and parents valuing what the school has to offer. This requires agreement on norms and expectations. Such alignment is a lot more feasible when everyone has chosen to be part of the school community.

And this is why school choice matters. It allows frustrated parents to seek out schools that actually want to serve their child, and empowers frustrated educators to create such schools. Just look at what's happened during the coronavirus shutdown, as large districts—with all of their rules and routines—have struggled to provide even minimal online instruction, with some hesitating even to require attendance. Meanwhile, less encumbered by routines and restrictive contracts, Success Academy and plenty of other charters have aggressively moved to remote learning that includes full instructional days, rigorous work, and attendance north of 90%.[8]

I'd be remiss if I didn't address one other weighty point you raise: whether choice hurts local district schools. I've three general responses: First, families who exercise choice are frequently dissatisfied with school safety or instruction, and I'm cool with unsafe, instructionally suspect schools enrolling fewer kids.[9] Second, contrary to the more overheated critiques of choice, it's not clear that traditional district schools even suffer financially when students depart. That's because funding structures designed to buffer these systems mean that even after they "lose" a student to a charter school or voucher program, they retain most of the local funds and some of the federal funds for that child.[10] Third, although I dislike the tendency to treat reading and math test scores as the measure of all things and think such metrics need to be handled with care, the research suggests that choice-induced competition has mostly led to gains in local district school performance.[11]

As we seek adaptive, creative responses to the coronavirus, I find myself far more optimistic about what we'll see from schools of choice than from districts nominally charged with ensuring that no student slips through the cracks—a promise that, as you note, so often goes unmet.

Best,

Rick

Dear Rick,

Well, my friend, you've raised important issues that make our exchange over choice so complicated. It is correct that many of the criticisms I make about choice and charter schools can be made about public schools. I often pointed this out while I was still in New York. Although many opponents of charter schools criticized them for failing to admit a proportional number of children with special needs or who are labeled English learners, the same critics were often silent when some public schools, usually those that serve affluent neighborhoods, were basically doing the same thing. As we both know, many magnet schools and specialized exam schools are essentially allowed to screen out the most disadvantaged kids.

So, I recognize that my argument has its limitations. However, my retort is: Why do we want to add to the existing inequities by creating *more* schools that screen out the disadvantaged? In your last letter, you acknowledged that at least some charters do this. We know that when we concentrate the neediest kids into a small number of schools, we significantly increase the likelihood that those schools and their children will fail. We see that pattern throughout the country, and No Child Left Behind did nothing to address this.

Again, I worry about the manipulation of parents in the charter sector and the parents who lack the resources to choose good schools for their kids. When state policies allow local public schools that serve poor kids to be underresourced, they often become overwhelmed by student needs and dysfunctional. In effect, we are writing off millions of children by relegating them to an inferior education.

Like you, I appreciate the innovation that I have seen some charter schools adopt, but honestly, most charter schools that I have seen aren't innovative at all. In fact, they are extremely traditional and un-exceptional. I like the flexibility that charter schools have when hiring teachers because it can make it possible to hire people who want to work with a certain population of kids. However, I remain concerned about schools that force teachers to work long hours and that rely on attrition because it keeps salary costs down.

I have visited many charter schools over the years, including the Success Academy Charter Schools in New York. Many of the Success Academy schools I visited were excellent, and although I am opposed to rigid discipline policies, I am even more troubled by chaotic, unsafe, and dysfunctional public schools that are horrible places for teaching and learning. I know I sound conflicted, but actually it is my honest assessment of what is happening, and it is why I refuse to generalize about choice and charter schools.

Here's the key issue for me: I believe that public resources should be used to support public schools and that there should be accountability for how public funds are used. Until policies are designed to ensure full transparency and to promote collaboration rather than competition among schools, I will remain skeptical that choice will not be used as a way to undermine our commitment to ensuring that all children have access to a good education.

Ideally, I believe access to a good school shouldn't be determined by where you live, whether you get a good lottery number, or whether you were willing to wait in long lines. Access to good schools is as important as access to the Internet, clean water, and safe neighborhoods. Do you think choice can take us any closer to this ideal?—Pedro

---

Dear Pedro,

Your concern about schools screening out the disadvantaged is compelling. In principle, I share your apprehension. In practice, though, things can get blurry.

Now, we agree on the need to always be on the lookout for unsavory actors (whether in traditional systems or schools of choice). So, there's a need for sensible regulation. That's why I support, for instance, requirements regarding auditing, financial transparency, criminal background checks for school staff, building inspections, and compliance with civil rights law. Where I grow more circumspect is when it comes to regulations that will restrict the ability of schools (like Success Academy) to set rigorous expectations or offer an effective learning environment.

Success Academy does indeed expect parents to accept its type A directives governing start times, parent–teacher meetings, student dress, and much else. Critics have suggested this is a scheme to chase away hard-to-serve families. I think that's nuts. Success Academy is offering those families that choose it a disciplined, rigorous, and demonstrably successful school model. Success Academy has judged that making this model work requires a partnership between family and school. That makes good sense to me. Now, it's not for everyone. Fair enough. But Success Academy's wait-list is long because it has thousands of students who are doing great and because tens of thousands of parents are hungry for what it's offering. Although the model may not work for every student or appeal to every family, that's no reason to deny it to those for whom it does.

That said, you're right that problems can arise when schools take public funds and then cherry-pick their students. So, why would we risk aggravating inequities by expanding choice? Well, practically speaking, affluent families already enjoy school choice—purchasing homes with an eye on the local schools or using private options. School choice programs matter most for low-income families who didn't get to pick their current school and aren't satisfied with the result. This is why I find worries about cream-skimming less than compelling. If anything, restricting choice mostly denies options to low-income parents. I think choice ultimately *advances* equity by empowering every parent to pursue options that work for their child.

You argue that most charter schools have done little to take advantage of their flexibility. I agree. Of the nation's 7,000 charter schools, I've long thought that not even one in five are actually taking advantage of the opportunities they enjoy. Whether due to inertia or a lack of imagination, most charters do indeed look a whole lot like local district schools when it comes to organizing the school day, utilizing staff, leveraging technology, and delivering instruction. To me, however, the fact that too few charters make full use of their freedom to serve kids is not an argument against choice but an illustration of why charter schooling alone is insufficient. This is exactly why I embrace an expansive vision of choice, including things like private school vouchers, hybrid home schooling, and education savings accounts: They open the door to a broader, more dynamic array of innovators and models.

Whatever my frustrations with charter schools, the larger point is that students have an enormous array of needs, preferences, and situations. It's often unreasonable to expect a single school, no matter how good, to effectively serve every child who happens to reside in a given geography. Choice provides options and allows for flexibility. The Great School Shutdown of 2020 has illustrated the point: Some students loved learning online at home; most didn't. Some parents liked home schooling their kids; many others felt overwhelmed.

In short, I think school choice's true allure is not a matter of the shortcomings of district schools but of what choice makes possible. Your point about school discipline, for instance, is a vital one. For me, it also brings to mind "Goldilocks and the Three Bears."

Here's what I mean: Nobody wants discipline that's "too strict" or "too lax." Everyone wants discipline that's "just right." The trick is that this means different things to different people, depending on the time, place, setting, students, backstory, and particulars. Asking districts to devise a single standard for all kids at all times is unreasonable, but so is telling parents to simply trust that their child is being disciplined fairly. Choice lets schools define "just right" and then allows teachers and parents to choose what works for them.

For me, that appreciation for the countless facets of human diversity is at the heart of choice's promise. What say you?

Best,

Rick

Rick,

Well, my friend, I find myself agreeing with much of what you've said in your last letter. As I mentioned, I have visited the Success Academy Charter Schools. In fact, on more than one occasion I was given a tour by the founder, Eva Moskowitz. I have no objection to much of what Success Academy is doing, except when there's evidence they're pushing out kids that are hard to serve. That big qualifier aside, I have encouraged other educators, especially those who are critical, to visit Success Academy schools. I think we can learn a lot from their thorough and comprehensive approach to education, and I give Eva credit for showing that you can create urban schools that serve poor kids of color well.

I agree that the Success Academy schools are not for every child, but why should we expect they would be? I see nothing wrong with parents who want a rigorous education for their child and who don't mind the strict discipline. If parents want single-gender schools, military academies, or career and technical schools, they should have the right to choose the option they feel will be best. As long as there is truth in advertising, and we admit that lots of kids, especially the neediest, may not thrive in these kinds of environments, then I can accept that.

You responded to my concerns about charters cherry-picking by arguing that students who attend schools of choice ultimately benefit. That may be true depending on the school, but I'm still concerned about the many more kids who are never chosen: the homeless kids, the kids in foster care, the undocumented kids, and the kids who don't have caring parents, or the kids raised by parents who are too disorganized to adequately support their children. We know what happens to these kids when they lack support and opportunity. Very few charter schools are designed for these types of children, and the schools that serve them are often underfunded and overwhelmed by their needs.

I saw this play out in New York City while Bloomberg was mayor for 12 years. I give him credit for never ignoring the schools, but under his leadership, the Department of Education closed over 140 neighborhood schools. They did succeed in creating several new, innovative schools, and some, but not all, were charter schools. But there were also neighborhood schools that had to accept the kids the other schools rejected. These schools that served the "over-the-counter" kids—kids who showed up after the school year began and registered over the counter—were more likely to fail because these students were usually behind academically and had other challenges.[12] Meanwhile, the screened schools and many charter schools never took these students, while those schools that did were more likely to fail.[13] In my opinion, this is unfair, and allowing it to occur is inhumane, unjust, and unsound policy.

Still, I might not be opposed to the concept of choice *if* it can be implemented in a fair and equitable manner. I haven't seen that yet, but I won't argue that it's impossible. Part of the reason why I remain open to the possibility that a fair and just system of choice can be created is

I would be a hypocrite if I opposed choice. The truth is, I have exercised choice at various times for all five of my own kids. They've all attended public schools, but I didn't just allow the district to decide where they went. I chose a bilingual school for the two oldest, but it turned out that it was neither good at teaching English speakers Spanish nor Spanish speakers English. So, for the next two, I looked for the schools that did the best job educating low-income children of color.

When I was a school board member in Berkeley, I picked which schools and which teachers my kids had. I knew too much about kids who slipped through the cracks to simply allow the system to make these decisions for me. While serving on the school board in Berkeley, I was shocked to learn that we had a school, Emerson Elementary, which had largely closed the achievement gap. I ended up picking this school for two of my kids. Although it had the same demographics as other schools in Berkeley, low-income Black and Latino kids were consistently outperforming their peers at other schools. Why? Strong leadership, a positive school culture, a laser-like focus on meeting student needs, and lots of parent involvement. I remember visiting the school on several occasions and watching the custodian, who was one of few Black male employees at the school. At lunchtime, he would throw a football with kids. When I asked the principal about this, she explained that they utilized every member of the staff to support kids. She also said that he was not merely a custodian, but a mentor. This made sense to me as did their focus on strong parent involvement and making sure that every student had an individualized learning plan. My question to the superintendent was: Why didn't the other schools learn from Emerson's success?

This is the question I keep asking. I don't care if it's a traditional public school, a charter, a magnet, or a private school: If it's found a way to successfully educate a broad variety of kids, we can learn from it. Seeing is believing, and the more we show that under the right conditions, all kinds of kids can learn, the more easily we will dispel the notion that because of race, poverty, culture, or language, some kids can't be educated.

This, in my opinion, is the real problem in American education. Racism makes it easy for so many to blame parents, kids, race, culture, or something else while we ignore the fact that America's inability to create schools where poor children of color are learning has more to do with our nation's history of segregation and unequal treatment than anything else. I see no evidence that choice will solve this problem. So, I remain skeptical of choice. I believe it's been sold as a panacea that will cure the problems that beset American education, especially among schools serving low-income children of color. Ultimately, I believe that when we look at nations such as Canada, Denmark, Holland, Barbados, Cuba, and Curacao, where children of color, especially Black children, outperform children in the United States, we see that when racism and poverty are addressed, educating kids ceases to be a big problem.[14]

Be well.—Pedro

CHAPTER 4

The Achievement Gap

For many years after the enactment of the No Child Left Behind Act of 2001, closing racial and socioeconomic "gaps" in student achievement served as the organizing principle of school improvement. The results, Rick and Pedro agree, were decidedly mixed. In this chapter, they discuss the causes of the achievement gap, how to address it, and how to understand the benefits and costs of a focus on "gap closing." Pedro starts by pointing to racially separate schooling, funding disparities, and the consequences of poverty as driving forces of the unmoving achievement chasm. He argues that "when we invest in poor children ... we can begin to reduce disparities in academic achievement." Rick agrees that targeted investment in programs with demonstrated results can have an impact, though he's dubious that hefty checks to struggling schools will make a big difference, absent other changes. More fundamentally, Rick believes that Pedro has offered only a partial diagnosis of the problem. Rick argues that family structure and individual behavior play a critical role, noting they are sensitive topics and thus hard to address, but makes the case that meaningful progress requires squarely confronting the role they play. Key themes include explanations for the achievement gap, potential remedies, and whether a focus on "gaps" is ultimately helpful.

Dear Rick,

I'd like to spend some time with you discussing the so-called "achievement gap." I preface the remark with "so-called" because the term has become quite controversial since it began being used with some frequency back in 2001 when No Child Left Behind (NCLB) was adopted. As a result of the law and the promises that accompanied it, the nation's gaze was cast toward reducing or eliminating racial disparities in student achievement. At the time, we were primarily focused on measuring achievement by disaggregating data by race and comparing student performance on standardized tests. It was hardly surprising that this way of framing the issue and measuring data exposed yawning gaps in achievement that corresponded to the race and class backgrounds of kids.

I say "hardly surprising" because we have known that there were huge disparities in funding and in educational opportunity for years. In fact, the existence of inequities in educational opportunity served as the basis for the Supreme Court's *Brown v. Board of Education* decision. Back in 1954, when the court unanimously decided that racially separate schools were inherently unequal, the court and President Eisenhower, a Republican war hero, understood that we had a system of apartheid in America that perpetuated and maintained racial segregation in schools and society. They hoped that by ending school segregation "with all deliberate speed," we might gradually begin to create a more equal society and begin to live up to our nation's noble ideals.[1]

Of course, the pace of change has been anything but deliberate, and we have never delivered on the promise or intent of *Brown*. Today, many of our schools continue to be characterized by a high degree of de facto race and class separation. According to a recent study by the UCLA Civil Rights Project, "Intensely segregated nonwhite schools with zero to 10% white enrollment have more than tripled in this most recent 25-year period for which we have data, a period deeply influenced by major Supreme Court decisions (spanning from 1991 to 2007) that limited desegregation policy."[2]

In addition to racially separate schooling, we have huge gaps in educational opportunity that are related to poverty. We both know that wherever poverty is concentrated, large numbers of students are struggling. For example, kids in 40% of school districts lack access to preschool, and many poor kids in low-income communities attend schools where no advanced placement courses are offered and where there are shortages of teachers who are trained to teach core subjects in math and science.[3] These kinds of disparities in educational opportunity are why many (myself included) have argued that we should rename the "achievement gap" an "opportunity gap." This makes it possible to draw attention to the numerous ways in which basic educational opportunities are denied to kids simply because of where they live.[4]

As a nation, we made our greatest progress in reducing racial disparities in achievement when we were most committed to fighting poverty. Remember President Eisenhower sent the U.S. Army into Little

Rock to enforce his integration order in 1957, and for nearly a year, the military was used to escort nine Black students to school because their safety was threatened by violent mobs. President Johnson went further and enacted programs like Head Start, the Elementary and Secondary Education Act, and a variety of War on Poverty programs to improve educational opportunities for poor children of color who attended racially segregated schools. Johnson himself was once a teacher who taught poor Mexican American children at a school near the Mexican border. I'm sure he understood from his experience that if we ignore poverty and limit our equity efforts to schools, the vast inequities in employment, housing, and incomes will undermine efforts to promote change.

We're a long way from that commitment now. Today, more than 50% of the nation's children qualify for free or reduced lunch, and nearly 40% of all kids come from families at or below the poverty level.[5] With few exceptions, every state spends more money per pupil to educate affluent children than it does to educate the poor.[6] Under these circumstances, I believe it is naive and unrealistic to think we will ever close the so-called "achievement gap." I say this not because I'm a naysayer or a pessimist, but because I'm a pragmatist.

How about you?—Pedro

Dear Pedro,

First off, we have real points of agreement. You're clearly right about the role that poverty plays in these disparities. I agree with your take on how the status quo closes the doors of opportunity to far too many kids.

You're also indisputably right to note how large the achievement gap has loomed over the past two decades. NCLB really did make "closing gaps" the organizing principle of 21st-century school improvement. The testing it required starkly illuminated undeniable, troubling disparities. That spotlight was long overdue and sorely needed. But I fear that NCLB also fueled a fixation on the short-term movement of reading and math scores, with unfortunate consequences for both equity and excellence.

We agree that institutional arrangements play a big role in producing inequitable results. In education, a big piece of this is the way that poor children get systematically trapped in dismal schools. And we need to explore solutions. As we've discussed, I think a big part of school choice's appeal is its ability to empower marginalized families whose children lack access to good schools.

For me, another key impediment to equal opportunity is degree-based hiring, which privileges the comfortable and connected in troubling ways (especially given the high-income, whitewashed demographics of college-goers).[7] After all, the college degree was never designed to be an employment test. If we're talking about degrees that reflect specific, essential skills—like in nursing or engineering—that's one thing. But the degree's modern role as a catchall hiring screen is a protection racket for campuses and affluent college-goers. The crazy part is that employment tests, which are less expensive, less arbitrary, and more direct gauges of embedded work tasks, are subject to a higher level of judicial scrutiny than are degrees.

Although we won't necessarily agree on the solutions, I think we can agree on the need to identify barriers to opportunity and then work to address them. All that said, I want to turn to an issue where I suspect we may disagree. Though race and spending surely play a role in the achievement gap, we need to acknowledge that a big part of the challenge is due to other factors that we're less comfortable talking about today—especially the role of family structure and individual behavior. Huge numbers of children today are raised in single-parent households.[8] As we both know, parenting is exhausting in the best of circumstances—and the challenges of helping school-age children navigate their education can all too easily tax the emotional, physical, and financial resources of even two-parent households. So, it's no great surprise that children raised in single-parent families are substantially more likely to drop out of school than otherwise similar peers.[9]

Please understand that I'm not talking about how much any parent loves their child and that I recognize there are plenty of two-parent families that do an awful job of rearing their kids—and plenty of single parents that do a phenomenal job. But the impact of family structure is a reality that intersects with race and class and contributes to the challenges we're addressing here. What I'm suggesting is that the marriage gap is a critical factor in explaining the achievement gap and that we need to tackle the first if we're serious about addressing the second.

Although this discussion inevitably raises issues of race and racial bias, it's equally crucial that we unapologetically address the role of individual choices and behavior—and not allow such questions to simply be subsumed by the discussion of race. The evidence is pretty clear, after all, that the racial differences in school discipline are due partly to disparities in how schools treat students but also partly to significant differences in student behavior.[10] Similarly, differences in academic outcomes and college-going are partly the product of structural forces but also of behaviors like student effort and study habits.

Though we can engage in epistemological discussions about the source of family structure and student behavior, it's tough to argue with the evidence that being raised in a two-parent household, developing disciplined study habits, and avoiding teen pregnancy dramatically influence life outcomes. After all, as Brookings Institution scholars Ron Haskins and Isabel Sawhill have documented in their book *Creating an Opportunity Society*, individuals who manage to follow three straightforward steps—complete high school, land a full-time job, and get married before having kids—have just a 2% chance of being poor.[11]

We need to acknowledge these simple truths and teach students accordingly. This should be done, I'd argue, in a manner that's respectful of communities and cultures, and with careful attention to which kinds of support, coaching, guidance, or assistance will actually help. In all of this, the overriding focus should be on what it'll take for students and families to make the most of these things.

Look, these are extraordinarily sensitive questions, so I want to be clear. I'm not suggesting we downplay America's racial legacy or questioning anyone's intentions. My point is that we need to proceed with eyes wide open. I've spent my career working to improve schooling because I believe equal opportunity should be an American birthright. That requires grappling fully with the role of racism and school funding but also with the role of individual choices and personal behavior.

With that, I want to turn to a related point, one where I'm quite curious to hear your take. I think it's a problem that we've been judging schools primarily by how well they erase achievement gaps. Indeed, I've long been concerned that 21st-century reformers got so intent on narrowing gaps in reading and math scores that they lost sight of the rest of the curriculum. I fear this has led schools to strip away so many of the things that make learning lively and engaging—like field trips, plays, discussions of current events, and science experiments. I suspect the impact may have been biggest on low-income students, who may be less likely to get those opportunities in their homes and communities.

In the same vein, too many school systems narrowed their focus not only on *what* they teach but also *who* they teach. The result was intensive test prep for students below the proficiency bar and benign neglect for students above it (accompanied by the cheerful mantra, "They'll be fine.")

Schools should equip every single child for citizenship and success. Systemic gaps that leave vulnerable groups of kids ill-prepared are a betrayal of the American promise. And yet I worry that our approach to addressing these gaps has been hobbled by the difficulties of talking candidly about all the challenges we face.

Best,

Rick

Dear Rick,

I'm fine with talking about "individual behavior" and the role of parents in supporting their children, although I don't believe this explains our racial disparities. Research shows that parent involvement at home is critical to improving outcomes.[12] However, many schools focus on getting parents involved *at* school. This form of involvement may be important, but obviously it is difficult for many working parents to do so. In my view, getting parents to demonstrate an active interest in their child's education when they are *at home* is even more important than whether they can be present at school during the day. I often point out that when we examine patterns of student achievement, typically the kids who receive the most support at home do the best in school.

So, we're in agreement about the importance of parents, but I find it odd that you would bring this up in reaction to what I said about the history of racial discrimination and state-enforced racial inequality in education. We both agree that history matters. We can't pretend that the *Brown* decision leveled the playing field, countered our history of structural racism, and created equal schools in this country. As I pointed out in my last letter, we continue to have blatant inequality in educational opportunities in schools that correspond to the race and class makeup of neighborhoods.

You see this in several states but most starkly in Illinois. There are hundreds of school districts in the state, some of which serve very few students. Those that serve the affluent typically have a lot more funding. For example, I recently visited the East Aurora School District in Chicago's western suburbs, where 97% of students are non-White and most are low-income. It spends $4,000 less per pupil than schools in the neighboring Batavia Public School District, which is 80% White and only 17% low-income.[13] Patterns like these are common throughout our country.

Typically, the only people who say that money doesn't matter are those who have lots of it. As we know, schools that have more money are able to pay higher salaries to teachers, have superior school facilities, and offer kids more electives and advanced placement courses. Affluent, college-educated parents want this for their kids, but so do low-income parents of all races. If we don't connect our discussion of the achievement gap with these pervasive forms of inequality, then I think we're being dishonest about our interest in closing the achievement gap.

I find it ironic that many conservatives who oppose affirmative action in college admissions because they regard it as an unfair racial preference are silent about the racial privileges their kids frequently enjoy in affluent suburban public schools and even more so in independent private schools. If we are serious about making sure the playing field in education is level and fair, we should look at the entire system, pre-K through high school, and not just simply college admissions.

Finally, you raised the point that, in their desire to eliminate the achievement gap, some schools have become more concerned about the performance of their lower achievers and ignore their high achievers. Based on my experience of doing research in diverse schools, affluent parents of high-achieving kids would never allow their children to be academically shortchanged in the name of equity. Generally, if affluent parents feel their kids are not receiving a good education, they take action. They will threaten principals and superintendents with their jobs or remove school board members. Unlike most low-income parents, they have the time and know-how to exert influence and pressure on schools, and school leaders typically respond to the pressure.

However, I imagine that there may be schools where the pursuit of equity has led to academic mediocrity, and where the curriculum has been dumbed down to meet the needs of lower-performing kids. If this is occurring, I agree that it's a big problem. All kids should be challenged, stimulated, and supported in school. It may be that some schools and educators think that when they serve a diverse student population, they must decide what level to teach at: low, medium, or high. It may also be that they simply do not have the resources to address student needs or provide more learning opportunities. Whatever the cause, when this happens, invariably someone loses out. Put simply, this is wrong.

The alternative is to differentiate, personalize, and tailor education to meet individual needs. This is not easy to do, but I have seen schools that do it quite well. For example, I was visiting an elementary school in Abington, Pennsylvania (one of the few districts that has made consistent progress in closing the achievement gap) and I saw that although some kids were reading *A Wrinkle in Time* in a 5th-grade classroom, others were reading Melville's *Moby Dick*. Having read *Moby Dick* myself, I knew how challenging it was. I asked the teacher why these students were reading such a difficult book in the 5th grade, and she said, "Because they can. I try to push all of my students." To me, this is exactly the kind of approach we should see in more classrooms: kids from diverse backgrounds being stimulated, challenged, and brought together to learn.

Although I think it would be better if the federal government and our society as a whole were committed to equity in educational opportunity and combating poverty, it would be a mistake to conclude that nothing can be done until this occurs. Schools like the one I described in Abington show us that it is possible to make a difference for all children, even under existing circumstances. I think other schools can learn from examples like these. What do you think about that?—Pedro

---

Dear Pedro,

Sorry to be slow in responding. Our eldest, Grayson, turned six yesterday. Trying to give a kid a decent 6th birthday while "sheltering in place" turns out to be a challenge. Who'd have thought? But the four of us had a pretty good time, and we found an hour of Skyping more congenial than I might've thought. Now, back to business. I appreciate your thoughtful response. As always, you make compelling points.

I wholeheartedly agree that too many schools and school systems fail to effectively serve their students. And far too many of these schools and systems are those serving low-income and minority students. Period. In the United States, given our tangled, oft-shameful racial history, these problems don't exist in a vacuum. You're right to note that they're the product of a living history that encompasses slavery, Jim Crow, racial profiling, and so much else. Whether or not we agree on particular remedies, we wholly agree that it's untenable and un-American that the doors of opportunity should be closed to even a single student.

Schools must be engines of opportunity. That has to be the expectation. This means they need to do better when it comes to guidance, instruction, and support, but as I argued in my last letter, success will also depend on students embracing their education and parents partnering with educators. To my mind, this isn't about casting blame; it's about being straight with students, parents, and ourselves.

Even our most ambitious policies haven't made nearly enough difference for students—especially for those left behind and on the wrong side of the gaps. We saw some narrowing of gaps in reading and math in the years following the adoption of NCLB, but those gains ceased in the 2010s.[14] The frustration with this plateau is widespread.

As you note, one explanation for the lack of progress has been the suggestion that we haven't adequately funded schooling. Some politicians and union leaders even claim that we've "defunded" public education.[15] I find such complaints unconvincing, given that after-inflation per pupil spending in the United States has roughly tripled over the past five decades and is among the highest in the developed world.[16]

Indeed, the role of school spending is one place where we see things pretty differently. I don't think the national data on school spending suggests that urban communities are systematically underfunded. Cities like Boston, Baltimore, Chicago, New York City, and Washington, D.C., all generally spend as much or more than their affluent suburbs. More than a decade ago, the Tax Policy Center, a partnership of the Left-leaning Brookings Institution and Urban Institute, examined per pupil spending by student race and found that "spending differences have largely disappeared" and that remaining differences are mostly "between rather than within states."[17] Indeed, in 2017,

Urban Institute researchers concluded that "poor students in most states attend school districts that are about as well funded" as those of nonpoor students.[18]

Qualifiers and queries are certainly in order, including the question of whether we should spend *more* money in low-income schools than elsewhere. That's all fair. But I just don't see the evidence that policymakers are shortchanging low-income, heavily minority school systems.

I'm certainly not saying that "money doesn't matter." Of course it can when funds are spent wisely and well. But when I see Newark or Trenton, New Jersey, spending well over $20,000 per student—close to *double* the national average—and still producing dismal results, I'm skeptical that a lack of spending is the big problem.[19] When the New York City superintendent pleads that he's slashed through "to the bone" while spending $28,000 per student a year—and after adding hundreds of positions to central administration—I question whether new funds will be well spent.[20] When I see Los Angeles spending a quarter or more of its school funds on teacher health care and retirement benefits, I'm dubious that more dollars will help in the absence of larger changes.[21] I'm open to spending more than we do but only if convinced the money will be spent in a manner that actually makes a difference for students.

If I'm lukewarm on calls for more spending, what do I think will help? One place I'd start is by seeking solutions that speak to a broader coalition for change. I think a lot of nominally "advantaged" families share the same frustrations you highlight—especially the concern that their children aren't being challenged or are being treated like test-taking automatons. Although I hear your point that affluent parents would never allow their kids to be shortchanged in the name of equity, I have observed that much of the suburban angst around testing has been fueled by a fear that their kids' schools have cut back on the things that make learning engaging, dynamic, and personal.

Perhaps the frustration has been driven more by middle-class families than the truly affluent, but it's certainly there. And it presents an opportunity: The fact that more and less advantaged parents have common complaints makes it possible to envision a broad-based coalition for change. I do think that social–emotional learning, personalization, career and technical education, and early childhood education tap into this in various ways, which helps explain their widespread appeal and current success.

I know we're on very different pages when it comes to school spending, but I wonder if you see us stumbling onto some patches of common ground here.

Best,
Rick

Hi, Rick,

I actually don't think we're far apart on some of the issues you raised. I agree that school funding is a complex issue and that we have to be more nuanced in how we approach it.

I will readily acknowledge that simply putting more money into failed school systems does not produce better results. For example, D.C. Public Schools has one of the highest per pupil spending rates in the nation, but it's questionable how poor kids benefit from this spending.[22] A few years ago, I was asked to work with a high school in D.C., not far from the Capitol. In fact, you could see the Washington Monument from the school. I attended a meeting with the school's administrators and was shocked when 25 members of the staff filled the room. I was surprised to learn that, in a school with about 600 kids, there were so many administrators and support staff. Several of the classrooms were staffed by two teachers, almost all of them from Teach For America.

Here's the problem: Despite all of the resources at the school, no one on the staff knew how to teach reading. Guess what? Many of the kids couldn't read! However, later that day I saw the marching band and was blown away. Not only could the kids in the band play music, they danced while they played and were invited to perform throughout the country. To my amazement, most of the kids in the band did not know how to play an instrument prior to coming to the school. Yet there they were, playing and dancing at a very high level. Of course, I asked the question: If you can teach the band to play like this, why can't you teach kids to read? As you might imagine, I wasn't invited back.

I think these are the kinds of questions we have to raise. I agree with you that we also have to ask: How is money spent? Money matters, but only if spent wisely.

At the same time, research shows disparities in school funding are real and pervasive.[23] There are a few notable exceptions, especially in some of the urban school districts such as D.C. and Newark, New Jersey, where spending is high and outcomes remain low. But the exceptions don't negate the need to acknowledge the allocation/funding gap. On the surface, it may seem as though these urban school districts receive equal or, at times, even more funding than suburban districts. But when we look closely at the data, we see that urban districts serve a much larger percentage on average of what we might call "high-need" kids: students with disabilities, kids in foster care, kids experiencing homelessness, English learners, and so forth.[24] These kids cost more to educate because they require more services. So, even if it looks like schools in D.C., Newark, or Baltimore are well funded, the dollars allocated really don't tell us how much it actually costs to educate their students.

Additionally, I can point to several studies showing that we allow far greater disparities in funding than most advanced industrialized nations in the world, including our neighbor to the north, Canada.[25] Schools serving poor kids in Toronto don't look like inner-city schools in the United States. They have great facilities, well-paid teachers, and their academic outcomes are a lot better. Race and poverty are not obstacles to achievement in Canada as they are in the United States.

I don't think we're in disagreement about the importance of public money in education. We may be in disagreement, however, about the need for strategic investments to accelerate learning from kids who are at a disadvantage due to poverty. We know that affluent parents typically spend lots of money on preschool, after-school, and high-quality summer programs. They do this because they believe that when they provide these types of opportunities to their children, it generally results in better outcomes in the future. In New York City, there are preschools known as the "Baby Ivies" because parents believe that if they get their 4-year-olds into these schools, they will be on the path to the Ivy League.

Parents from low-income communities typically can't afford high-quality preschools. However, the Harlem Children's Zone in New York City has shown that when we invest in poor children with preschool, health care, music lessons, and so forth—the very types of supports that most affluent families readily provide to their children—we can begin to reduce disparities in academic achievement. The question is: How do we generate the will to make strategic investments in children common in more places?

Happy birthday to Gray!!–Pedro

Dear Pedro,

"If you can teach the band to play like this, why can't you teach kids to read?" Hah!! That would make one helluva title for a book about school improvement. And I'm afraid I'm unsurprised that you weren't invited back. Those kinds of questions can be immensely uncomfortable–and the default response is to expel the person who dares to ask them.

In general, there's more agreement here than I might have imagined. You're right that affluent parents spend money on all kinds of things–from preschool to summer camps–that those with less money can't afford. These things matter. And we do indeed want school buildings for every child to be attractive, safe, and well maintained; it's a travesty when kids are packed into dirty, decrepit buildings. So, I'm on board with targeting extra resources to serve low-income students, as we already do with Title I and state funding formulas. Of course, as I've said before, that's contingent on my conviction that those funds will be spent effectively. Thus, although I'm generally supportive of the Harlem Children's Zone and similar efforts, I'm more skeptical of sweeping proposals to have Uncle Sam shovel more money into schools and programs.

You ask about building support for more strategic investment in poor communities. As we've discussed, evidence that dollars are actually having an impact can help make the case that new spending will help actual kids and won't just serve to subsidize suspect bureaucracies. I also tend to think that emphasizing the importance of providing opportunities to every single child and focusing less on tackling "gaps" is more likely to win broad public support. Such a message sounds more like, "Let's provide this for all of our children," and less like, "Let's boost spending for those kids over there." I think the first of those two always plays better in the United States.

One of the compelling things about the Harlem Children's Zone is, as you note, that it focuses on a lot more than reading and math scores.

We do well to gauge progress at tackling "gaps" by focusing on a more comprehensive set of outcomes. Looking to a broader set of metrics can help resist the temptation to narrow instruction or shortchange advanced subjects, civics education, or the arts.

In your last letter, you suggest that the real issue with funding isn't that urban schools are shortchanged but that equity requires more be spent on educating low-income children. I find this point more compelling than the underfunding argument that you'd alluded to a little earlier. It's a reasonable point, resting on the same logic underlying Title I or weighted student funding. Although I support targeted funding for low-income students or children with special needs, I'm hesitant to embrace a doctrine that makes a policy of purposefully shortchanging middle-class students. After all, though schools have too often stiffed low-income students, I can't think of anyone who's suggested that was good policy. I just don't think enshrining a two-tiered vision of school funding as accepted practice is the right way forward.

More generally, I've often found that the debate about school spending feels cartoonish. Some public school critics seem to bizarrely suggest that "money doesn't matter" in education, whereas those championing more spending often come across as cavalier about how those funds get spent. I'm convinced that education leaders and policymakers could help tremendously on this count if, when making the case for more funds, they made it a point to document how dollars are being spent and to explain what they're doing to ensure that schools are getting good bang for the buck. And, between you and me, I'm puzzled by the fact that they so rarely do.

We come at this work with different experience and perspectives. And yet even on a fraught topic like this one, I'm struck that we've found several patches of common ground when given the chance to share our thoughts and sift through our differences. That's a reassuring thought as I contemplate what we want for my boys, your kids and grandkids, and tens of millions of their peers.

Be well, my friend.

Best,

Rick

CHAPTER 5

Testing and Accountability

If school choice is the most divisive topic in education, testing is a close second. Yet Rick and Pedro, who've frequently been on opposite sides of the accountability debates, find much common ground when it comes to the strengths and shortcomings of testing. They agree that schools should be accountable for serving students well and that testing has a vital role in shedding light on student outcomes and helping teachers in their work. They then pivot to a discussion of the problem with putting too much weight on reading and math tests and why so much No Child Left Behind–style testing was unloved and unhelpful. Pedro endorses Rick's notion that "testing is valuable because it measures whether students have mastered the content and skills they need to learn" and then makes the case for portfolio assessment, though Rick cautions that portfolios have their own weaknesses and can be vulnerable to some of the same pressures that plagued testing. They agree that more needs to be done to help persistently low-performing schools, though neither claims to know how to consistently or confidently drive such improvement. Major questions include how much reading and math tests should matter, whether schools are measuring the right things, and what ought to be done when there's evidence that a school isn't effectively serving its students.

Dear Rick,

We were just talking about the achievement gap and once again identifying some of the areas where we agree and disagree. It seems like whenever we get into a discussion about the achievement gap, we invariably begin discussing test scores and their significance. So, let's talk about testing and how it's been used since the adoption of No Child Left Behind (NCLB).

Under NCLB, most states were testing kids each year. In fact, in several states, as new standards were enacted, they even tested kids on material that hadn't been taught. In effect, they put more emphasis on assessment than on teaching, which seems odd; it's a bit like weighing yourself to see if you've lost weight, without having gone on a diet or increased your exercise. This approach to testing led to quite a bit of pushback from many teachers and parents, and in some states it contributed to the movement to "opt out" of testing entirely. Although I've been critical of the way we have used standardized testing, I should point out that I have not encouraged parents to opt out of testing. I think that is a decision that parents should make on their own.

Personally, I don't identify as an anti-tester. I think there can be value in assessment if we use it as a tool to guide learning and not merely for the purpose of ranking kids, teachers, or schools. I think we need to know how much students have learned, how well prepared they are when (or if) they graduate from high school, and how to diagnose their learning needs when they struggle academically. I once heard former secretary of education Rod Paige say that we could eliminate the achievement gap if we simply stopped testing kids because we would no longer know how well they were doing. I believe he was making a valid point.

There's no question that test scores illuminate important disparities. In my own research, I rely on test scores at an aggregate level to analyze patterns among schools. We recently released a report on the state of Black children in Los Angeles County to try to understand why the test scores of Black children had been flat in recent years. Our work pointed to the numerous disadvantages these children experience outside of school (e.g., high asthma rates, homelessness, and foster care placements) as factors contributing to underperformance in school.[1] Without the test scores, we would not have even known where to look.

However, Paige and other advocates of high-stakes testing miss something very important. It's not good enough to know how well students are doing on tests. If the tests provide useful information on what kids need to know, then it's even more important that we know how to respond when we see clear evidence that they lack skills and their academic needs are not being met. NCLB failed miserably in this regard.

Under the Every Student Succeeds Act (ESSA), states now have more flexibility to determine how frequently they will test and what they will do to ensure accountability. I have worked as an adviser to several states—New Mexico, California, Washington, and Oregon—that are looking for alternatives, so I know from experience how complex the issues are. Even the most ardent anti-testers recognize the need to assess kids so that we have a clear sense of how much they have learned. However, no state, in my opinion, has devised an effective strategy for responding to schools and districts that struggle to generate growth in student achievement, especially in high-poverty districts.

This is really the big issue: How can schools mitigate the effects of poverty so that when students are assessed we obtain an accurate sense of what they can do? We know that kids whose basic needs—food, shelter, health care, and so forth—have not been met generally don't test very well. We also know that schools serving large numbers of poor children are often overwhelmed by the needs and challenges facing the children. Reducing the frequency of testing will not solve this problem. Simply telling schools we already knew were struggling that they are failing is not effective policy, in my opinion.

So, what are your thoughts on this?—Pedro

Dear Pedro,

Testing is so divisive because it's so crucial. After all, it touches on the central question of schooling, namely: What do we want students to learn? As you make clear, that instantly raises complex issues of who is learning, what constitutes adequate learning, and what we should do about schools where students aren't learning.

Let's start with your observation that no state has developed effective plans for systematically helping struggling schools to improve. I think, generally speaking, that you're right. And yet as I see it, this doesn't mean accountability is unhelpful or unimportant. Asking people to be responsible for their actions is the foundation of any social contract. I want my kids to be accountable for their decisions and behavior. I want Apple to be accountable for whether my iPhone works. I like the fact that I'm accountable for what I write and say. And I certainly think that accountability is called for when it comes to public schools spending public funds to educate the public's children.

Nearly two decades ago, I penned a piece for *Educational Leadership* titled "The Case for Being Mean." In it, I observed that accountability can be invaluable for its ability to press leaders to reexamine how work is organized and resources are used.[2] A focus on results *can* spur leaders to revisit comfortable routines and pursue painful but necessary changes.

That said, I don't think that's how accountability has played out in schooling. In fact, several years later, I penned another piece for the same magazine about what test-fueled leadership had wrought. The title? "The New Stupid."[3] My frustrations encompassed the kinds of problems you point out, including a lot of brute force test preparation and energetic efforts to grade schools and teachers with test scores. We saw far too little leadership devoted to rethinking how schools work or what teachers do.

In the testing era, we've relied too heavily on tracking convenient reading and math scores. We've done so, in part, because we seem to have lost sight of just why it is we care about tests in the first place. Testing is valuable because it measures whether students have mastered the content and skills they need to learn. Although literacy and numeracy matter a good deal, they're poor proxies for all that we want students to know and do. Yet rather than focus on finding valid and reliable ways to measure more of the outcomes we care about, policymakers and pundits, researchers and reformers developed tunnel vision around the couple of numbers we could readily quantify. It often felt like parents and teachers were the only ones with qualms about any of this.

After all, reading and math are only a piece of what we want students to learn in school. Yet we treat those test scores as proxies for pretty much everything else—to the point where we routinely use "good school" as shorthand for a school that has high reading and math scores, and "effective teachers" as a label for teachers whose students have high reading and math scores.

Again, test scores matter. I care a lot about how well students can read and how proficient they are at math. But I fear these scores are limited, imperfect tools that got stretched beyond their breaking point. Reading and math scores are most useful for those outside of schools— like public officials and advocates—who want a simple, straightforward measure of performance. That's fine. That kind of gauge has real value. These blunt metrics are of much more limited utility, though, when it comes to changing what happens inside the schoolhouse. More useful for improving instruction or school routines are finer-grained measures, like what share of class time is devoted to instruction. In my experience, unfortunately, these other things are too rarely tracked, even at schools celebrated as "data driven."

I suspect all of this has a lot to do with why parents may choose to opt their children out of standardized testing. Like you, I've never counseled anyone to opt out or told them that they shouldn't. Although that call has to be a parent's prerogative and will depend on the particulars of the situation, I think that the hostility with which so many reformers regarded "opt out" was telling in its own right. Reformers seemed unable or unwilling to grasp why a parent might want to opt their kid out of an 8-hour assessment. I kept hearing opt out denounced as little more than a product of "privilege" or "union misinformation." Reformers would splutter, "Parents take their kids to the pediatrician and the dentist, so what's the problem here?"

What got lost, I think, is that pediatric visits run more like 30 minutes; involve personal, real-time feedback; and entail parents talking with a live medical professional about how to address any issues that emerge. In short, a pediatric visit is almost nothing like taking a state assessment, which yields impersonal, unintelligible state data 6 months later. In fact, if we thought about how to make educational assessment more like visits to the pediatrician, parents and teachers might start to view testing rather differently.

I look forward to hearing your thoughts on all this, my friend.

Best,

Rick

Rick,

I have to agree with you on this. The complexity of the issue makes it hard for me to take a simple pro or con stand on testing. This is another one of the reasons why the polarized debates that are common in education circles are so unhelpful.

On the one hand, I'm concerned that standardized tests can give an unfair advantage to the most wealthy and privileged students. Today, I was asked by a journalist to respond to a faculty committee that recommended that the University of California Board of Regents not abandon the SAT as a key criterion for determining admission.[4] That's good news for the College Board, which makes tons of money from the SAT and AP tests, but is it good for students? I think not. We know that many kids attend schools where they are not well prepared for the SAT and don't have access to the test-prep courses that can be quite expensive. Moreover, because the SAT is an aptitude test rather than a criteria-referenced test that's based on what kids were actually supposed to learn in school, it's easy for students who receive tutoring and so become good test takers to benefit at the expense of others.

The problem is: What's the alternative? Grades are not necessarily better predictors of future college performance, and there are many schools, especially those that serve affluent kids, where grade inflation is rampant.[5] Finding a way to evaluate students that's truly fair is not easy, but I don't think placing so much emphasis on the SAT or ACT is the answer.

With respect to the standardized tests that kids take in 4th and 8th grade (and often much more frequently in some states), I agree that assessments should provide more personal, immediate feedback. The medical analogy you brought up in your last message is a useful one. When we go to the doctor, tests are often used to provide the patient and the doctor with a sense of how healthy they are. The results are not used for the purpose of ranking. If your blood sugar and blood pressure are high, it's a sign that you may need some intervention to stay healthy.

I think we should approach the achievement gaps identified by testing in the same way.

As you note, when schools test kids, the information we collect is often not used to help kids. In fact, we typically test the kids in the spring and give teachers the results in the fall when they no longer have the same students. Assuming the results are accurate—and that is a tricky assumption because we have no way of knowing whether or not a student was tired, sick, or simply didn't take the test seriously when sitting for the exam—why shouldn't we use the results to inform how and where students need more help?

One possible alternative to using test scores exclusively is to evaluate students via portfolios that collect samples of student work over time so that teachers can identify areas where support is needed. Schools using this approach can clearly see whether or not a student can write, read, problem-solve, or do research based on what they actually produce. This seems fairer and more reliable to me as a way to ascertain what kids have learned.

So, I have more questions than answers on this one, but I know states are looking for solutions to the problems that tests reveal. Unlike academics who have the luxury to simply ponder hypotheticals, those in positions of leadership must make decisions, and they are likely to be held accountable by the voters for the consequences of their actions. They're looking for help. What do we have to offer?—Pedro

---

Dear Pedro,

You nailed it. It's so much easier to say, "This is complicated!" than to offer useful guidance. (I suspect that's why I spend so much time saying, "This is complicated!")

But you're also right about the need for practical answers. The University of California has to decide which students to admit. Policymakers have to figure out which schools are doing a responsible job of educating kids. Teachers have to figure out whether children have learned the things they're supposed to learn.

On the college admissions front, I think tests have a role to play as a comparable, consistent barometer. They can serve as an independent check on things like grade inflation, connection-fueled letters of recommendation, and the biases of admissions staff. At the same time, as you rightly note, the SAT or ACT can certainly advantage students with access to tutoring. What I think you give short shrift, however, is that tests like the SAT can also serve as a powerful equalizing force. After all, the whole reason for the creation of the SAT a century ago was to help ensure that students who lived in the "wrong" communities, didn't have connected parents, and attended the "wrong" schools would still have a chance to prove their mettle.[6]

As far as K–12 policy goes, I believe that state testing plays a useful role. Although I thought NCLB was a case of ham-fisted accountability, it's also true that some schools perform woefully year after year. Especially when it comes to basic skills, we need to know how schools are faring and whether they're improving. That's one big thing that I think Every Student Succeeds Act (ESSA) got right in 2015. It retained the testing and transparency requirements of NCLB while sharply curtailing Washington's role as far as telling states which schools were "failing" and what should be done about that.

When it comes to the actual work of teaching and learning, "testing" strikes me as integral. Now, in the hands of veteran teachers, "testing" may not look a lot like a test. For example, a teacher may ask a student about a short story to assess how well she understood it. That's a "test" of a certain sort. Teachers are constantly gauging what students know and don't know, why they're confused, and how best to instruct them. It's a problem that this kind of useful, low-key formative assessment has gotten swamped by the excesses of the accountability era.

And that brings us to portfolios. In theory, like you, I love the idea of portfolios. In practice, though, I can't help but remember the research from Vermont in the late 1990s that found that there was no agreement from one teacher to another when they scored student portfolios.[7] The grade depended almost entirely on who was grading it, which gets us back to the concerns about capriciousness that arise when we talk about basing college admissions entirely on things like grades, essays, and interviews.

In fact, it's not hard to envision the same problems that bedeviled testing playing out in the case of portfolios. Donald Campbell famously coined "Campbell's law" nearly a half century ago, cautioning that metrics become less reliable as they become more important. When results start to matter, people start feeling pressure to cheat or take shortcuts. That's why NCLB so quickly led to concerns about test prep, manipulation, and chicanery. It's all too easy to see how these same pressures could play out with widespread, mandatory portfolios. Unfortunately, I just don't think we yet have the ability to do portfolios fairly and rigorously on more than a piecemeal basis.

Where does that leave us?

We seem to agree that testing has a valuable role as an independent check and as a monitoring system. We're both concerned that many of the assessments that we focus on aren't pedagogically useful and that an important question for policy and practice is how they could be. We both see the allure of portfolios, though I find myself concerned about their practicality.

I'm hoping you can help me figure out where we go from here.

Best,

Rick

Dear Rick,

Thanks for the thoughtful response. I can see clearly where we agree, but I'd like to push you further on a few points. If we agree that the goal of testing should be diagnostic and to provide useful information on how well students or schools are doing, then what do we do when we see clear evidence that schools are not performing? In my opinion, this is the biggest problem. We know that simply labeling a school as "failing" and threatening to fire the principal or teachers does nothing to help a school improve. Closing failing schools or having the state take them over also has a terrible track record. In fact, I know of no state that has done this well.

I think there's an alternative, and it's one that I've encouraged several states to adopt. In his book *Coherence,* Canadian education policy expert Michael Fullan has written quite persuasively about the progress achieved in Toronto through professional capacity building over the past 20 years.[8] Put simply, when the Ministry of Education in Ontario sees clear evidence based on assessments that a school is struggling, rather than apply pressure, they send targeted help. For example, if they see that students are struggling in math, they send trained math educators to the school to work with teachers in teaching math. They operate on the assumption that if the kids are struggling in math, they have to help teachers become more effective at teaching it.

This sounds logical but it's not what most states in the United States do. Here, we use threats and pressure as a change strategy. At one point not long ago, every large urban school district in New Jersey had been taken over by the state. For example, Newark and Patterson were under state control for many years, but what did that accomplish? The same occurred in California, in Inglewood and Compton. Most of the districts that have been taken over predominantly serve Black and Latino children, and there's no evidence that schools improved as a result of state control.[9] The pressure created by this form of accountability is driving lots of good educators out of schools where they're needed or out of the profession entirely.

I've seen the capacity-building approach work at some schools in the United States, and I think it could be applied on a broader scale *if* the states develop the capacity to actually help schools. That's a big "if" because most states have been organized to hold schools accountable and to make sure they are compliant with various state and federal policies. Few states have the expertise to actually help schools, but there's no reason why they couldn't develop it. I believe by shifting the direction of policy in this way, we will make it clear that assessment can indeed be used as a tool rather than a weapon.

The state of California is trying to do this, but it's too early to see if it will work. They're directing more resources to schools serving large numbers of disadvantaged kids, but so far they have not given them any guidance on how to use the funds. They're also calling on schools to reduce suspensions but haven't been clear about what alternative forms of discipline should be used. I think we must do more to provide concrete guidance and support to schools, but I think California and a few other states may be moving in the right direction.

Be well.—Pedro

Dear Pedro,

Your note has me thinking that if we'd devoted half as much energy to making assessment useful as we have to formulaic debates about whether testing is "good" or "bad," we'd be in much better shape. This, of course, requires that we be clear about what it means for tests to be "useful." On that score, we seem to have unearthed a whole lot of common ground.

You know, I expected the back-and-forth on this topic would be pretty intense. Yet it feels like we've just waded through one of the most divisive questions of 21st-century education without finding much fundamental disagreement at all. We both see the value of testing in principle but have grave concerns about how it's played out in practice. I'm left wondering whether the real flash point here has been misunderstood. Perhaps it's less between the Left and the Right and more a clash between those caught up in the promise of accountability and those more inclined to see its practical travails.

I'm sure plenty of accountability hawks were legitimately shocked when analysts finally got around to documenting the staggering amount of time that schools were devoting to testing and test preparation.[10] The backlash felt like a political dispute, with progressives blaming NCLB and conservatives the Common Core. The bigger story, though, was that after a sensible idea ran wild, the reformers who'd fought for testing got defensive when parents and teachers pushed back. An opportunity for constructive course corrections turned instead into an ugly melee.

These things are always hard to see in the midst of the storm. By the time we finally can see them, it can be too late. That's got me wondering how we can do better going forward. On that score, this exchange has surfaced a few thoughts.

First, when it comes to instruction, assessment and diagnosis are part and parcel of good teaching. Good teachers assess all the time and in all kinds of ways, formal and informal. The problem is that testing for learning has gotten steamrolled by testing for accountability; we've prioritized tests that are useful to public officials rather than those that are useful to parents or educators. A much larger share of assessment should be devoted to advancing student learning, not just auditing it.

Second, we shouldn't simply trust schools to do their thing any more than we should blindly trust police departments to do theirs. As I've noted, public schools spend public funds to educate the public's children. Public servants should be accountable, and that starts with transparency. The reality is that too many schools aren't doing their job as well as we'd like, and too many students are getting lost along the way. Regular state testing is important for illuminating how all learners are doing and providing some baseline accountability.

Third, this leads to the question of what to do when we're convinced that schools must improve. NCLB's answer was its infamous cascade of mandated remedies. That ham-handed approach failed dismally and prompted a healthy pullback in ESSA, which retained the transparency but ditched the mandated "interventions." As you point out, that begs the question of what should be done to "fix" struggling schools. On that count, after observing decades of mostly disappointing strategies, I fear I have no simple or straightforward answers. (And it's probably worth noting that no one else really does either—the private sector, for instance, boasts its own pretty dismal record of turning around struggling businesses.)[11]

This is a massively unsatisfactory state of affairs. There are too many schools where too many students are struggling. Part of the answer undoubtedly involves your call for "capacity building"; there are certainly times and places where support, training, and more resources will make a big difference. But I've also seen lots of low-performing schools spend a lot of money in ways I find ineffectual or wasteful. In such cases, I doubt a blank check and hand-holding will help. That's when I look to the kinds of structural changes provided by school choice, for-profit delivery, or attempts to reimagine the teaching profession.

In the end, I keep musing on the role of testing in medicine. In health care, we don't see much resistance to checkups or cancer screenings. In fact, tens of millions each year take these tests voluntarily. That's because we trust that they're being used to identify practical problems, that they're only collecting what's necessary, that doctors will know what to do with the results, and that there's a direct link between the test results and our doctors' ability to treat our illnesses. If we spent more time asking what it would take for testing to look more like that in education, I suspect our long-running debates would start to look very different indeed.

Best,

Rick

CHAPTER 6

Social and Emotional Learning

Although it might seem obvious that schools should focus on making students feel safe and valued, Rick and Pedro argue that the importance of doing so was too often lost amid the test-driven excesses of the No Child Left Behind era. When it comes to social and emotional learning (SEL), they find much to agree upon, starting with the conviction that SEL is a healthy reminder that schools need to tend to the "whole child." As Pedro observes, "It seems like common sense to acknowledge that we cannot separate a child's academic needs from their social, emotional, and psychological needs." Yet, for all SEL's promise, Rick and Pedro both caution that the tough work of cultivating social-emotional growth can turn into a slew of one-off programs that overburden teachers, distract schools from academic learning, or fuel problematic practices. Rick adds his concern that too many advocates seem inclined to blur the lines between SEL and a broader ideological agenda, a prospect he finds troubling but one that Pedro doesn't regard as a significant concern. Critical issues include what to make of the current enthusiasm for SEL, how schools can best approach students' social-emotional needs, and what it will take for SEL to successfully deliver on its promise.

Dear Pedro,

So, let's talk social and emotional learning (SEL in the common parlance). Personally, I'm a big fan of the logic behind SEL. It brings us back to the social mission of schooling that we've discussed previously. There's obvious value in helping students forge healthy relationships and make responsible decisions. This seems pretty intuitive. In fact, when we talk about SEL, I find myself wondering, How did we ever get to the point where it's a big deal to note that children learn better when they feel safe, valued, respected, and supported?

As we've discussed previously, we got here because No Child Left Behind's (NCLB) earlier, well-intentioned insistence that students should be able to read and do math eventually morphed into a bizarre exercise in *Office Space*-style management, one where it increasingly felt like students were being treated as cogs in a giant test preparation machine.

During the NCLB era, we gave short shrift to making sure students felt safe and valued. There was too little emphasis on cultivating skills like impulse control and persistence, or even on teaching students to respect and listen to one another. SEL offers the opportunity to rectify that while putting brain science to work and promoting vital virtues like integrity, empathy, and responsibility. Pretty much a win-win.

After all, as we've discussed, teachers and schools have been tasked with both teaching content and cultivating character since the dawn of the republic. Seen in that light, support for SEL is really just a reminder that schools should unapologetically embrace both academic achievement and the social and emotional skills that equip students for citizenship, life, and work.

I can't think of many parents who have a quarrel with any of the foregoing in principle. That's why SEL is so easy to love and could be such a unifying force. But SEL's widespread popularity also means that this push could all too readily morph into another goofy craze.

I fear there are too many vendors, consultants, and ideologues who see SEL as an invitation to displace content instruction, burden teachers, or pitch dubious pedagogy. Cheerful talk of "quality training" won't solve the problem that many teachers may have no idea how to cultivate persistence or that some of what's being pitched is pseudoscientific junk.

I can't help but recall, for instance, the "self-esteem movement" of the 1980s and the way it morphed into an attack on academic rigor. After starting out with the reasonable claim that students learn better when they believe in themselves, this high-profile push went off the deep end. It soon devolved into complaints that grading and demanding classwork threatened students' self-esteem, leading to lowered expectations and content-free pedagogy. This is why I get nervous when SEL enthusiasts mock the relevance of content mastery in the 21st century or suggest that the ubiquity of Google has made mere content knowledge akin to a frivolous party trick.

For me, so much of the promise and peril here is encapsulated in "restorative justice," which—as you know better than I do—approaches school discipline by eschewing punishment in favor of teaching students to treat one another respectfully. In theory, I love the idea. And when done carefully and well, it can be a terrific approach. The problem is that I've heard from far too many teachers and parents who've experienced it being done clumsily in their schools, sowing chaos, making teachers and students feel less safe, and creating a culture in which students issue insults and threats without consequence.

In short, I want to see SEL work in practice, not just in theory. I'll be curious to hear how you see things.

Best,

Rick

Dear Rick,

It's clear we agree on a lot here, though my take is a bit different on some of the issues you've covered.

First, I'd like to echo your thoughts about the irony of treating SEL like a new idea. To me, it seems like common sense to acknowledge that we cannot separate a child's academic needs from their social, emotional, and psychological needs. Such separation has never been feasible, and it's good that we are finally remembering that there's more to education than how well kids do on standardized tests.

I also agree that NCLB is largely responsible for the narrow focus that many schools adopted in the last several years. We urged and pressured schools to focus narrowly on academic achievement, and too many interpreted this as ignoring the other needs kids bring with them. Like you, I saw many schools drop or reduce art, science, physical education, and a host of electives because kids weren't going to be tested on these subjects, while doubling up on math and literacy. I think we both agree that kids need a well-rounded education. This is why I think focusing on the "whole child," even if it sounds awkward, makes so much sense.

I was just visiting a school in Lynwood, California, that has infused the arts into the entire curriculum. Kids are singing, drawing, playing music, and acting while they write, problem-solve, and learn history and science. It's great to see how motivated and happy they are. This shouldn't surprise us. Kids learn better when they're happy and when we teach them in ways their brains are hardwired to understand.

This is what SEL and the whole-child focus is intended to do. Consider this: It used to be common for every kindergarten teacher to have a piano in the classroom. We used to recognize that music was a great foundation for learning. How many kids do you know who have memorized the lyrics to hundreds of songs? What does this tell us about the ability of music to help kids retain information and to motivate them to learn?

However, like you, I have concerns about how well SEL is being implemented in schools. For example, I too fully support school systems that use restorative justice, but like you, I have seen schools that do this quite poorly. They treat restorative justice as a new technique for discipline and fail to see that it must be accompanied by a shift in school culture; a focus on developing character that is rooted in basic values (e.g., honesty, integrity, discipline, empathy, etc.); and a commitment to building strong, positive relationships that promote learning and child development.

I think many schools struggle because they are accustomed to relying on disciplinary responses such as suspensions rather than addressing the root causes of misbehavior. Ironically, many schools suspend kids who don't even like school. It's as if they think staying at home to watch television or play video games is an effective deterrent to bad behavior. If kids are acting out because they don't understand the material and feel embarrassed, sending them out of the room or suspending them will not address the problem. We must try to address the cause of behavior problems if we hope to change behavior.

I will raise one additional concern: I worry that the SEL push may be asking too much of teachers and schools. It's not reasonable to expect a teacher who is trying to cover content and teach skills to also act as a social worker or surrogate parent.

However, although it might seem appropriate to tell schools to focus on academics, we're living at a time when this may not be reasonable. We are in the midst of a mental health crisis throughout the country. Large numbers of kids, many of whom are affluent and high achievers, are depressed, anxious, and alienated. According to a recent study by the American Association of Family Physicians, one out of six American children suffers from a mild to severe mental illness.[1] We're also seeing a rise in suicide rates among all groups, and as we both know, fears related to shootings at schools are at an all-time high.[2] Given these trends, it seems almost unavoidable that schools take on responsibilities beyond academics.

Let me leave you with this question: How do we make sure that we are not setting schools up to fail by asking them to take on so many challenges?—Pedro

---

Dear Pedro,

I'm hard-pressed to find anything in your letter with which I'd take issue.

I'll start with where you ended. You're right. We do indeed overburden schools by treating them like magic Band-Aids. Whatever problems we identify, *someone* sees schools as the solution—demanding yet another program, priority, or policy. Each asks educators to slice their time ever more finely and makes it that much harder for them to do anything really well. That risk is one big reason why schools can't do this work alone but need to tackle it in partnership with their communities, including youth groups, health professionals, and churches. The work of SEL is something that teachers can't be expected to do on their own, even those fortunate enough to get useful training and support.

I also think you're absolutely right about the promise of a "whole-child" approach. It's a hugely appealing notion. After all, a real education involves rigorous academic preparation and art, science, physical education, and more. Good schools are attentive to all of that. At the same time, I tend to bristle at the phrase itself, having been in far too many conversations where it was suggested that being for the whole child means one *must* be for this additional budget request or that faddish program. It can all wind up feeling more like a lobbying strategy than an educational vision.

I share the concerns you've raised regarding implementation. If there's anything that decades of school reform have taught us, it's that even good ideas are only as good as the execution. This is where research and evaluation can be especially helpful. To be sure, measuring and tracking things like emotional control and civility can be tricky, and I worry about slapdash efforts to evaluate these things. But social scientists have developed a wealth of metrics to gauge things like civic engagement and tolerance and it's important to explore how such tools can be used to document the impact that SEL efforts are actually having.

Lastly, for me, the essential SEL insight is the need for children to feel safe, valued, and connected. I think public opinion turned so sharply against NCLB because parents felt like test-driven schools were losing sight of this. Parents saw testing delirium up close and started to worry that their kids were getting lost in the shuffle. After all, parents instinctively appreciate that children learn best when they're interested and engaged. That's why art, music, poetry, and play are essential to the fabric of schooling—they speak to us as thinking and feeling beings, a truth that's near the heart of iconic educational treatises spanning from Plato's *Republic* to Rousseau's *Emile*.

This little riff on parents, the arts, and the classics brings to mind the issue of faith and religious tradition. Indeed, as Marilyn Rhames, veteran educator and founder of Teachers Who Pray, observes, there's "no place in education where the impact of religious faith is more evident than in social-emotional development."[3] I've long been struck that the SEL skill set can be traced pretty cleanly back to the foundational virtues and morals taught by just about every faith. Yet the advocates and researchers who've led Team SEL don't see it that way, approaching their work as a matter of cognition, programs, and technical acumen. In fact, Rhames says faith is so "conspicuously absent" that she terms it SEL's "f-word."

And the issue isn't one of constitutional law, as the Supreme Court has made clear that working with churches or religious groups alongside other community partners accords with the First Amendment's establishment clause. Rather, the issue here is one of comfort level and culture. Although tens of millions of Americans are going to view the stuff of SEL through the lens of faith, the coastal funders, education researchers, and cosmopolitan advocates who've led the SEL push tend to see things pretty differently. I don't know quite what to make of this tension, but I am sure that it deserves a lot more attention than it's received.

It feels like we're very much aligned on this one, my friend. Given that, I'm curious what you think lies ahead.

Best,

Rick

Dear Rick,

We certainly do agree on the goal, so perhaps we should proceed to focusing on how schools should do this. After all, implementation is often where things get messy and sometimes fall apart. I can think of lots of good ideas that have been implemented poorly (e.g., block scheduling, project-based learning, advisories, etc.) and were abandoned by some schools, though clearly not all. The question is: Can schools address SEL while simultaneously supporting their academic needs?

To me, when SEL is implemented successfully, it has been embedded into the culture of the classroom and the school itself. In our best schools, this happens organically. No one has to tell teachers to get to know their students or to develop positive relationships with them. It happens as a normal part of the educational process. However, in schools with very large class sizes, or where there are strained relationships rooted in racial or cultural differences between adults and kids, a focus on social and emotional learning may be interpreted as an imposition, yet another thing we're asking schools to do that distracts from their main goal: academic learning.

Educators have to be shown that, far from being an extra, SEL makes it possible to achieve the main goal of enhanced academic learning. For example, how do you run successful science labs in which kids are required to work in teams, if kids haven't learned how to work together? If they don't know how to listen and respect each other, how to work out conflicts when they arise, or how to collaborate, a science lab or any group project is unlikely to be successful.

This is why it's essential that teachers establish norms in their classrooms for how we will work with, speak to, and treat one another. Ideally, students should have input into the establishment of these norms so that they have a sense of shared ownership and responsibility. Lawrence Kohlberg reminds us that norms and the values that underlie them are ultimately more important than rules because rules are only as good as our ability to enforce them.[4] What we should be after is getting kids to internalize values like respect, integrity, honesty, and so forth. This has to be modeled by adults and reinforced constantly so that it becomes a part of the school's culture.

This is why SEL is so hard. A commitment to social and emotional learning requires buy-in from adults. If the staff doesn't believe in it, it won't be taught, modeled, or reinforced, at least not consistently.

A brief example may be helpful. I was visited by a new middle school principal in New York City who wanted my help. She explained that every day at lunchtime, her students were having food fights, and despite her efforts to stop them, they continued. She was at her wits' ends. My first response was: Why did you come to me? Do I look like an expert in handling food fights? She explained that she was afraid to let someone in the central administration know about her difficulty because she was new to her position and school. She said, "They'll probably tell me that if I can't stop food fights, I shouldn't be a principal."

I understood her dilemma and agreed to help her. I did this by taking her to visit another middle school not far from hers. There, she witnessed kids eating together family style: One kid gets the salad and brings it to a round (not rectangular) table; another gets the entrée. They eat together and then clean up after themselves. Lunch is a pleasant experience, and at several tables we saw members of the staff eating with their students. The new principal was impressed. When she asked the principal at the school we visited what made it possible for lunch to be such a pleasant experience, the principal explained that the school had once been quite dysfunctional, but she had worked closely with her staff, parents, and eventually students to create a culture throughout the school that not only influenced how students ate lunch, but the learning environment in classrooms as well. Although the principal, Nyree Dixon, was only 32 years old when she was assigned to lead PS 8 in Brownsville, Brooklyn (one of the few neighborhoods in Brooklyn that has not been gentrified), she had won over staff, parents, and students to a vision rooted in a belief that together they could create a school where students were safe, supported, and academically challenged.

I share this story because I have found that too often, school leaders pay insufficient attention to school culture when trying to address issues like discipline. I know that it might not have been easy for the new principal I brought to visit PS 8 to change the way they ate lunch at her school, much less change her school's culture. However, I felt it was important for her to see that such a positive culture could be created. It was especially important that we visited a school in a similar neighborhood serving a similar population of kids. I think that when we get better at showing educators how to do things, whether it be SEL, formative assessments, or project-based learning, we are more likely to see improvement.

What do you think?—Pedro

Dear Pedro,

"If you can't stop a food fight, you shouldn't be a principal." Now *there's* a mantra that should be shared early in the orientation of every principal training program.

You put your finger on something that we've all seen: school cultures where teachers and leaders hesitate to voice uncertainty, confusion, or a need for help, and with good reason! When I do trainings, I get the clear sense that too many teachers and leaders have learned that asking for help—or flagging a problem—is seen as an admission of incompetence. It's hard to think of anything more certain to stop educators from learning or schools from improving.

How do we do better? For starters, we need to make it safe for educators and would-be reformers to admit what they don't know. Although there are certainly schools that do SEL well, I see little evidence to support the claims of those who say they've discovered the formula for doing SEL effectively at scale. Indeed, when confronted by those who insist they know what works, it's good to keep in mind the disappointing track record of school improvement strategies that we've discussed previously.

In any event, I suspect that doing SEL effectively begins with leaders willing to reimagine how schools go about their work. Quick-hit professional trainings or half-baked programs aren't the answer. Rethinking demands time, space, and a culture that accepts stumbles as the price of creative problem solving.

All this may just be another way of making your point that school culture is at the root of SEL. Like you, I think that effective SEL needs to be grounded in a school's everyday practice. Our mutual friend, Harvard's Jal Mehta, put it well once when discussing a deeper learning collaborative he hosts that includes educators from both the United States and Canada. He told me that, when it came to SEL, the Canadian educators were inclined to say, "Yep, this is just part of what we do." The Americans? They kept wanting to talk about new programs and interventions.

I'll share one final qualm because I'm curious to hear what you think of it. I've found that a nontrivial portion of the SEL community seems to view its work in ideological terms. I recall being part of the luncheon panel at arguably the nation's preeminent annual SEL conference, along with a Democratic presidential candidate and a dec-orated scholar. The nominal topic was what it would take for SEL to succeed and how to keep it from getting politicized.

Given the topic, I found it ironic that our panel was preceded by three speeches from high school students that would not have been out of place at the Democratic National Convention. The students gave short, impassioned speeches on immigration and gender. They lambasted Republicans, urged the audience to become allies, and showed not a whit of empathy for the notion that some listeners might see things differently. They were greeted by cheers and wolf whistles.

The issue was not the sincerity of the students' passion or the value of their voices. The issue was that the conference organizers and attendees didn't see anything objectionable about this commingling of culture war, policy advocacy, and SEL. They seemed to think that a commitment to SEL implied that one opposes the enforcement of immigration laws, supports schools defining sex in terms of gender identity rather than biology, and believes Republicans are wicked. Look, I'm all for teaching kids values like empathy and respect, but if support for SEL means endorsing a partisan agenda that I find wrongheaded and mean-spirited, I'm out.

Best,

Rick

Rick,

I agree with your critique of quick-fix interventions. Most educators understand that there are no simple or easy fixes to complex problems. This is why I'm optimistic about the focus on SEL. Many educators already understand the need to build relationships with kids. Once they get permission to stop focusing narrowly on test prep, we might see more teachers focusing on creating a climate in their classrooms where kids feel known, cared for, and challenged.

Education has been ridden with fads and driven by policy gimmicks for too long. By now we should know that there are no easy answers and that technical solutions must be accompanied by shifts in culture.

Let me close this with one more anecdote. I was contacted by a reporter a while back who told me about a school on the border near

San Diego (Edison Elementary) where nearly 100% of the kids are from families in poverty and over half are English learners. Despite these demographics, nearly three-fourths of the kids are at proficiency or higher in math and literacy, and this has been the case for several years.[5] He wanted to know how I might explain such an accomplishment. I told him that even though I had never seen the school, my guess is that it has to do with the culture: strong supportive relationships between students and teachers, parents and teachers, and among the students themselves. It turns out, that school's principal and several parents said the same thing.

We have lots of research on how to support teachers to be more effective, but much less on how to transform the culture of schools. This is why I think it's so important to learn from schools like this one, even though replicating what they have achieved is not easy.

I don't want to suggest that we can ignore poverty or blame schools that face similar challenges and aren't as successful. However, this should serve as a reminder that when SEL is integrated with a clear and coherent focus on teaching and learning, great things are possible.

More to come, my friend.—Pedro

CHAPTER 7

Civics Education

In an age of grave concerns about the state of civil society, civics education is very much in the public consciousness. Today's youth have access to a world of social media that provides a front-row seat to fierce culture clashes regarding issues of race, gender, climate change, free speech, religious freedom, and more. In this chapter, Rick and Pedro quickly agree on the need for a more rigorous, robust, and engaging approach to history and civics. Significant differences soon emerge, though. Rick expresses his concerns about what he sees as a tendency to forgo a richer, more complex narrative of American history in favor of an emerging new orthodoxy rooted in a caricature of American villainy. For his part, Pedro emphasizes the importance of not running away "from the controversies or the 'ugly side' of U.S. history"—including the founding fathers' shameful entanglements with slavery and the exploitation of Black and native peoples. In the end, Rick and Pedro come back to a shared conviction that balancing a clear-eyed view of America's shortcomings with an appreciation of its profound strengths is crucial to the future success of the American experiment. Key themes include the goal of civics education, how schools should teach students to think about citizenship, and how educators should approach the American story.

Dear Pedro,

As two once-upon-a-time social studies teachers, we've both had a lot to say about the state of civics education. We've commiserated that too much civics and history teaching seems like a blind sprint to get from the Revolutionary War to Vietnam. The result is instruction that's rote and reductionist, when it should be an exploration of the world-changing events, extraordinary figures, and compelling questions that make up the American story. This is nuts. At a gut level, we all know how vital civics education is to the health of our communities and our nation. This is where we teach students about how we've gotten here, what it takes for self-government to work, and the rights and responsibilities that come with being an American.

Our current struggles are on display every time we see new evidence about how little Americans know about our government, the Constitution, or our history. I mean, the University of Pennsylvania has reported that just 26% of Americans could name the three branches of government.[1] The Woodrow Wilson Foundation found that only one in three could pass the nation's citizenship test.[2] It's really pretty shocking. After all, the genius of the American system is its ability to evolve, to channel passion and partisanship into constructive channels. This only works, though, if Americans know how to actually use that system.

The goal, as I see it, is not knowledge for its own sake. Knowledge is, however, a precondition if students are to ask crucial questions, examine them, and make up their own minds regarding the answers. After all, it's hard to constructively debate what equality, opportunity, liberty, or justice require in law enforcement or social policy unless one has a clear sense of what these ideas mean, the historical context, and the facts in dispute. That's why a grounding in American history, civic life, and government is so important.

At this juncture, of course, things get complicated. For many years, educators, scholars, advocates, and parents have wrestled with questions like, Whose history gets taught? Many have worked to make civics instruction more illuminating and informative by expanding its scope and emphasizing people, events, analyses, and perspectives omitted from the old "generals and presidents" narrative.

I'm on board with these changes. Students need to understand how our institutions look from the perspective of those who couldn't vote or who were locked out of opportunity. Students need to be versed in Jim Crow and the World War II internment of Japanese Americans to understand the principles of liberty and equality, and how we have too often failed to uphold those ideals.

But I worry that too many in this discussion are less interested in forging a richer, more complex narrative than in a new orthodoxy built around a caricature of American villainy. To my mind, much of this derives from the problematic legacy of Howard Zinn and his imitators, especially their contention that American history is little more than a parade of horribles. They see an unbroken litany of graft, hypocrisy, and oppression.

This would constitute a cartoonish, unserious history in almost any land, and that's particularly true in the nation that brought (however imperfectly) the principles of liberty, equality, and democratic government into the modern world. Indeed, as Mary Grabar has pointed out in *Debunking Howard Zinn*, Zinn had an unfortunate habit of omitting inconvenient events and misusing historical sources in the service of his larger thesis.[3] Yet, this school of thought is influential in progressive circles and schooling today. Indeed, the *New York Times'* Pulitzer Prize–winning and widely adopted 1619 Project, which claims that the United States was founded as "slavocracy," seems committed to building on this disconcerting legacy.[4]

I believe that, for all of our nation's failings, Americans have been bequeathed a priceless gift. Indeed, I'd argue that our shared history is a messy but empowering tale of struggling to live up to our founding ideals. That tension is the beating heart of the American story. Students need to understand how unique our land really is: a sprawling, multiethnic society that's stable, democratic, free, and immensely prosperous. They need to learn how significant America's tradition of free speech, free press, and free assembly truly is. They need to appreciate what so many have sacrificed to promote justice, expand liberty, and face down external threats. In short, students need to study America's failings but also need to see them in perspective.

I tend to suspect that we disagree about the way in which I characterize Zinn's contributions. I'm interested to hear how you view his work and where you'd push back on my qualms.

Best,

Rick

Dear Rick,

I knew Howard Zinn (he and I spoke at a rally at Harvard in support of fair wages for campus workers in 2001). I was a fan of his book, *A People's History of the United States,* and drew upon it when I taught social studies.[5] What I loved about it was that it presented U.S. history from the perspective of those who have been left out: Blacks, Native Americans, women, workers of all kinds, and so forth. Zinn never saw his work as a replacement for other texts but as a supplement that could provide a richer and more complete picture of U.S. history.

Like you, I don't think we should run away from the controversies or the "ugly side" of U.S. history. In fact, I think they make history more compelling to students. On the one hand, I think it's impossible to deny that the United States was founded on slavery and the genocide of indigenous people. The enslavement of African people and the conquest of indigenous lands generated tremendous wealth for landowners. Most of the "founding fathers" owned human beings that they used as slaves to enrich themselves and build this country. Learning about the violent displacement of the Cherokee on the "Trail of Tears" forces students to see that Native Americans were subject to relentless violence and begins to erase the myth of Thanksgiving that we were taught in school. This is why the 1619 Project is so important, even if it is disturbing to many White Americans.

This does not mean that the democratic ideals reflected in the Constitution are not important. In fact, they have served as a source of inspiration to freedom-loving people throughout the world, including the people of Haiti who created the second independent republic in the Western Hemisphere after defeating the French and liberating themselves from slavery in 1803. One of the reasons why I enjoyed Lin Manuel Miranda's *Hamilton* so much, despite criticism that he glossed over slavery, is that aside from the great music and lyrics, he captures the contradictions of American history in a powerful way. Washington, Madison, and Jefferson were slave owners *and* advocates for democracy and freedom. I think it is important for students to understand how both could be true.

When students are forced to grapple with the meaning of freedom and the complexity of history, I believe they are better prepared to participate in democracy. In my teaching days, I once staged a debate with my students over whether or not Black people were better off free or enslaved. Learning about what life was like after the Civil War; finding out that Lincoln and others seriously considered repatriating Black people to Africa when slavery ended; and understanding the rise of the KKK, the prevalence of lynching, and the pervasiveness of White violence toward newly freed Black people is important for all kinds of kids, but especially for those who are White. This type of understanding of civics better prepares students to understand the racial justice movement that has swept the country as a result of the police killings of Black people.

Like you, I believe, I don't think the goal of teaching civics or history should be to produce patriots. I think it should be to produce critical thinkers who are ready to actively participate in democracy and defend their rights and freedoms when they are attacked.

Can I get an amen on that, Rick?—Pedro

Dear Pedro,

I should've figured you'd know Zinn—it often seems like you've known pretty much everyone! We'll have to make time some day for a fuller conversation about Zinn and his legacy.

In any event, you're incontrovertibly right that big parts of the American story are troubling and should be taught accordingly. Issues of slavery, religious intolerance, racism, sexism, and exploitation are an integral part of that "richer, more complex narrative" I mentioned in my last letter. For all that, I fundamentally disagree with the notion that the nation was "founded on" such things. This comes down in part, I suppose, to how we make sense of the hypocrisy implicit in slaveholders having helped found the modern world's first democracy. But it's also a matter of how we understand the American ethos and teach it to our children.

The United States was founded as an experiment in profound idealism at a time when liberty and equality were still regarded as novelties. Birthing such a nation in the 18th century required compromises that today seem sordid. But, for me, the telling point is that our founding ideals, documents, and institutions have been used to help rectify and redress many of those unsavory compromises and to steadily expand the scope of freedom. To teach our children otherwise is to urge them to devalue the priceless legacy they've inherited and to weaken the resolve required to redeem America's full promise.

We agree that the goal is not mindless patriots. The aim is to teach students to be reflective and grapple with the meaning of freedom and the complexity of history. That said, I do wonder whether what you describe as the goal of civics education—namely, preparing students to participate in democracy and defend their rights and freedoms—is sufficient. Absent an appreciation for the sacrifices so many have made, I fear it's all too easy to fixate on our nation's failings while looking past its remarkable gifts. I don't want mindless patriots, but I do want students to learn that they are part of the American story, they should value the legacy they've inherited, and they have a critical role to play in shaping our shared future.

I think Eliot Cohen, dean of the Nitze School of Advanced International Studies at Johns Hopkins, put it best when he recently observed:

> Particularly for Americans, patriotic history is a kind of glue for an extraor-
> dinarily diverse republic. Lincoln used a patriotic version of the revolutionary
> past and the founding generation to hold the Union together and provide
> meaning and redemptive hope to the slaughter of hundreds of thousands in
> the Civil War. . . . Civic education requires knowledge of history, not only to
> know whence conventions, principles, and laws have come, but also to de-
> velop an attachment to them. And civic education is also inextricably inter-
> woven with patriotism, without which commitment to the values that make
> free government possible will not exist.[6]

This is all front of mind as we lurch through the coronavirus crisis, the national shutdown, and the protests triggered by the police killing of George Floyd. In times like these, our ability to answer the challenges rests on our ability to work together, trust one another, and make shared sacrifices. The fact that we've seen such division and stumbled so publicly is, to me, one more reminder that we need to do a better job of nurturing a shared sense of community and belonging.

Now, I'll reiterate that this is not a call to downplay America's failings or to excuse cheerful BS about cherry trees. The goal, as I see it, should be to wrestle frankly with the good and the bad in the American story while teaching students that we're all part of the American family.

I guess I'm left wondering whether, and how, we might nurture the "patriotic" bonds of community and belonging without seeking to create jingoistic "patriots"?

Best,
Rick

Rick,

I'm glad that we're in agreement that the goal of teaching civics and history should not be to produce patriots but, as you said, to "be reflective and grapple with the meaning of freedom and the complexity of history." I also agree that it is important for students to see how they are connected to the "American story," as long as that story is not based upon lies or partial truths. I agree with the sentiments of the late John Lewis, who in an op-ed published after his death wrote, "Democracy is not a state. It is an act, and each generation must do its part to help build what we called the Beloved Community, a nation and world society at peace with itself."[7]

I believe that seeing democracy in this way is important because it lets our students know that they have a responsibility as citizens to be involved in the ongoing effort to create the "Beloved Community" and a more just society. As we both know, social studies textbooks in the past were written in a way that whitewashed our history. I didn't realize until I was in middle school that almost all of the founding fathers were slave owners. I'm not sure when children should learn this bit of history, but when I found out about it, I felt cheated. It felt as though I had been lulled into admiring leaders like Washington, Jefferson, Patrick Henry, and others without being given a full picture of who they were. Although it may not make sense for them to be judged by modern standards of morality, it is important to recognize that even by 18th-century standards most of them knew slavery was wrong. This is why Washington promised to free his slaves upon his death (although his wife Martha reneged on the arrangement when he died).[8]

In short, schools that don't teach all aspects of history unjustly deprive their students of the important opportunity to grapple with the full story of their country.

Aside from debating how history should be taught, though I think we both agree it is a debate worth having, I am concerned about how values such as pluralism and tolerance for differences are conveyed in schools. We may disagree about how to teach students about racism, but I think we can both agree that the current rise in racism, anti-Semitism, and White supremacy poses a threat to the social order and to our democracy. Hate crimes are up throughout the country, and Nazi groups that once operated in the shadows now feel emboldened to hold marches and spread their hateful ideas online and in print. The killings at the Tree of Life synagogue, the racially motivated shooting at the Walmart in El Paso, and the Unite the Right rally in Charlottesville that resulted in the killing of a counterprotester are all ominous signs. Reasonable people can disagree about immigration, affirmative action, or climate change, but when we treat those we disagree with as enemies and seek to silence them through violence, then we are all in trouble.

I think the way we teach civics should be unequivocal on the issue of tolerance. We should teach our students how to disagree respectfully and how to debate intelligently using evidence rather than threats of violence to support their views. Democracy and the social contract that holds us together as a society depend on our ability to do this.

To quote one of our most famous slaveholders, Thomas Jefferson: "If a nation expects to be ignorant and free, in a state of civilization, it expects what never was and never will be."[9]—Pedro

---

Dear Pedro,

You're spot on when you note that "we should teach our students how to disagree respectfully and how to debate intelligently."

We see eye to eye on the importance of tolerance, in principle. Schools should cultivate understanding and mutual respect. Students need to learn that reasonable people can disagree and that it's vital we be able to hash out those differences constructively and respectfully.

Yet, in practice, I've too often seen my progressive friends try to silence ideas they dislike in the name of "tolerance." For instance, as I've said, I believe that parental responsibility and student behavior must be part of any effort to close achievement gaps. When I say this, some on the Left ignore the substantive argument and summarily denounce me as a racist undeserving of a public platform, all under the banner of their supposed "tolerance."

Similarly, the agents of "tolerance" have made clear that the wrong kinds of thoughts regarding school discipline or history instruction can be deemed "problematic"—reserving for themselves the right to determine just what the boundaries of tolerance entail. And I'm no longer even surprised when I see self-professed paragons of open-mindedness in academe who want a scholar investigated or sanctioned for having the "wrong" views on Title IX enforcement, gender identity, or assertions of systemic racism.

Again, I believe in tolerance. But tolerance can't be a matter of creating safe spaces for those who agree with us. Look, I get that many in education will disagree with me on all manner of things, large and small. I've got no problem with that. I'm fully prepared to accept heated disagreement and harsh criticism. The avatars of "tolerance" should be, too. That's fundamental to democratic debate and to healthy self-government.

Heck, George Washington was subjected to vicious slanders. Thomas Jefferson regarded it as a badge of honor that the young nation was willing to tolerate royalists in its midst. As Jefferson would argue in his first inaugural, even those who wanted to dissolve the new union should be allowed to "stand undisturbed as monuments of the safety with which error of opinion may be tolerated, where reason is left free to combat it."[10] That's part of the American creed. But the champions of tolerance have to be sincere about that conviction. "Tolerance" must be more than a rhetorical, partisan ploy.

I find these issues particularly stark in the national dialogue around race. You poignantly note the threat posed by racism and White supremacy. We agree. Period. I do think there's something worth adding, though. I suspect that one reason the incidence of "racism" and "White supremacy" can seem to be growing is that advocates have developed a troubling habit of wantonly labeling views with which they disagree as "White supremacist."

I recall when protesters at Harvard University attacked U.S. secretary of education Betsy DeVos as a "White supremacist" because she supported school vouchers.[11] Now, DeVos had worked for decades with Black and Latino leaders and spent millions to help Black and Latino families access better schools, and even her critics didn't allege that she'd said anything that qualifies as racist. If she's a White supremacist, it seems to me that the term has lost all meaning. I have no beef with those who disagree with her on school choice or criticize her performance as secretary of education. But I don't see where "White supremacy" enters into any of this, except as a convenient way to try to stigmatize her and delegitimize her voice and views.

What say you, my friend?

Best,

Rick

Hi, Rick,

I agree with you on two of the things you said in your last letter. First, we throw around charges of racism and sexism too often and without substantiation. To accuse someone who supports standardized testing of racism makes the accusation seem ridiculous. I disagree with Secretary DeVos on many things, but I have seen no evidence that she's a racist. I have met many Black educators and parents in Michigan who saw her as an ally. Although I disagree with DeVos on vouchers and think the way she used her philanthropy to further a narrow, pro-charter agenda has ended up damaging educational opportunities for children in Detroit and Flint, most of whom were poor and Black, it doesn't mean that she did these things because she hates Black people. As a wealthy person, her view of what poor Black children need may be paternalistic and wrong, but calling it racist isn't helpful, in my opinion.

This relates to a larger problem in American politics: the tendency to demonize people who disagree with us. I think that tendency is adding to the polarization we're seeing now throughout the country and adding to the toxicity of American politics. The debates in education have been plagued by the same sort of extreme positions and tendency.

I also agree that we should work harder to get parents involved in supporting their children and that there's nothing racist about saying so. In fact, I think it's patronizing to assume that because parents are poor, don't speak English, or have limited education, they can't help their kids to do well in school. Neither of my parents graduated from high school, but all six of their kids (me and my siblings) graduated from college. I know that not all parents can support their children the way mine did, and I'm not using myself as a standard for others. This is why I never blame parents for not doing more to help their kids. I know that most parents love their children but may lack the means or know-how to help them. When schools blame parents for not doing more to support their kids, it creates yet another barrier between schools and the communities they serve. This is the opposite of what Nyree Dixon did at PS 8 in Brooklyn. She engaged parents to create a culture that supported learning.

Bringing this discussion back to the question of civics and social studies and their role in preparing kids to be citizens in a democracy, perhaps it might be useful to discuss how we teach it if we want to develop critical thinking and instill values such as tolerance. Earlier, I wrote about debate as a useful pedagogical tool.

But I think we can go further than just suggesting a few pedagogical tools. I agree with you that we can encourage students to be active in their communities and to engage with the issues that affect them. I work with some schools now that teach kids to do research on issues that affect them in their schools, community, society, and the world. The issues they examine can be as mundane as litter or traffic, or as complex as immigration and climate change. What I find most promising is that they not only learn about how politics and policy shape the way these issues affect them, but they also are encouraged to devise a plan for addressing the issue. This might include presenting an issue before the school board or city council, or it might involve educating residents about the need to consider alternative forms of energy. The goal is to get students to see the need to become actively involved in the democratic process. To me, this is much more important than simply encouraging people to vote.

I think that if students can see how they can apply what they learn to improve their lives and society, they might take what they learn more seriously and be a whole lot less bored in their social studies classes. This is what I tried to do when I taught American history to high school students years ago. As two former social studies teachers, I think we'd both agree that would be a welcome change.—Pedro

CHAPTER 8

For-Profits and Privatization

In this chapter, Rick and Pedro tackle the hair-raising issue of "privatization." After allowing that he may be one of the few souls in education who is actually enthusiastic about the role of for-profits and privatization, Rick suggests that many who are critical of these things misunderstand their meaning, applying the terms far too liberally. Rick posits that education would be better off with a balance of public, nonprofit, and for-profit actors. As he puts it, "For-profits and privatization don't represent any kind of an educational elixir. But I do think they have a valuable role to play." Pedro, on the other hand, is skeptical that the private sector should be entrusted with the public's funds. Instead, he points to New York City's publicly operated subway system, which brings together New Yorkers of all walks of life, as an example of a unifying, democratic vision for schooling. Both Rick and Pedro view the profit motive as a double-edged sword, agreeing that it can incentivize cost cutting while necessitating oversight—but they ultimately see that trade-off in very different ways. The major questions include how to think about "privatization" and whether for-profit providers can bring distinctive strengths to schooling or constitute an unacceptable assault on public education.

Dear Pedro,

In education, few words set as many teeth on edge as the term "privatization." Let's dive into that. It's a term that can mean many things. Indeed, I find that plenty of ardent "anti-privatizers" use the phrase to refer to a lot of things that, well, don't involve "privatization" in any conventional sense.

"Anti-privatizers" have described teacher evaluation systems, alternative teacher licensure, and school accountability as privatization. The phrase is even used to refer to philanthropists *giving away* money (which is kind of the opposite of making something private). To paraphrase Inigo Montoya from *The Princess Bride*: "I do not think that word means what the anti-privatizers think it means."[1]

The reforms denounced by "anti-privatizers" may or may not be good ideas. They certainly alter bureaucratic routines. But, whatever else they are, they aren't acts of privatization. Privatization is "the transfer of a business, industry, or service from public to private ownership and control," if you don't mind my quoting the Oxford Dictionary. Evaluating teachers, changing licensure rules, and holding schools accountable for test results may be a lot of things, but they aren't privatization.

Now, there is plenty of education reform that does involve privatization—and I broadly support it. In fact, I think it's good to have for-profits involved in schooling, and I generally support expanding their role. Although I'm happy to see for-profits supply books and buses, I'd also like to see them play a larger role in the actual work of schooling.

I know this stance strikes many in education as heresy, so I'll say a bit more.

First off, I'll readily acknowledge that for-profits have plenty of flaws. But the same is true of public systems and nonprofits, and the flaws (and strengths) of these sectors are distinctive in ways that make them useful complements. For-profit organizations certainly can be motivated to engage in selfish, troubling behavior. But the public sector, too, has incentives that can fuel selfish, troubling behavior, a fact painfully familiar to anyone who's ever seen the meanness of school leadership or the dysfunction of school boards up close.

Moreover, I'm pretty fond of the profit motive. I reject the premise that it's a bad thing. In fact, I think it can be enormously healthy. For-profits have reason to relentlessly seek out cost efficiencies, even when those are uncomfortable or unpopular. Public and nonprofit managers, on the other hand, have less to gain from productivity increases, more cause to fear public or philanthropic blowback, and thus more incentive to tread gingerly. In schooling, productivity gains can translate into smarter use of staff, less administrative overhead, more parental support, or better-maintained facilities. All of these things can be very good indeed for kids and communities. Pressure to grow revenue means that for-profits have cause to expand rapidly, allowing them to serve more students faster.

For all their cheerful talk about innovation and mission, nonprofits and traditional school districts often hesitate to become "early adopters" of cost-saving changes when they threaten to annoy influential constituencies or upend familiar routines. Even big, well-known education nonprofits, like brand-name charter schools, grow far more slowly and show much less inclination to squeeze their costs than do comparably successful for-profit ventures.

For-profits are also able to tap the equity markets, which means promising ventures can gain access to the resources they need without having to woo foundation staff or legislators. Revenue streams generated by paying customers mean that for-profits are less subject to the short attention spans of funders or the ebbs and flows of policy. I always enjoy talking to the CEOs of thriving tutoring or educational software companies because they're blissfully removed from the intense attention to donors and grant opportunities that tend to dominate conversations with nonprofit executives. In short, I'm not trying to apologize for for-profits or say "I don't hate them"; rather, I'm arguing that there's a lot to *like* about for-profits.

The fact is, private companies *already* play a tremendous role in public education in ways that draw hardly any notice. Although the "anti-privatizers" rail against nonprofits like Teach For America (TFA) and against democratically elected legislators deciding to alter teacher evaluation, I rarely hear many complaints about the massive role that private firms play in building schools, operating buses, supplying desks and laptops, or delivering professional development.

Of course, that may just be conceding the obvious, because it's hard to imagine how you'd run schools in the United States without buying goods and services from for-profits. That's kind of the point, though, isn't it? While the nation has been on lockdown and schools have been shuttered this spring, we've had steady access to food, water, electricity, clothing, and hand soap stocked on local shelves—or even delivered to our doorsteps—due to the endless adjustments made by for-profit enterprises. We shouldn't be too quick to dismiss that.

I want to be straight: The record of private ventures in education, as elsewhere, is plenty mixed. I don't mean to romanticize for-profit education, which certainly has its share of sleazebags and dubious characters. The incentive to cut costs can translate into a willingness to cut corners. The urge to grow can lead to deceptive marketing. These are legitimate concerns, and they call for appropriate transparency, oversight, and regulation.

For-profits and privatization don't represent any kind of an educational elixir. But I do think they have a valuable role to play.

Best,

Rick

Dear Rick,

You've opened up several controversial issues with this topic. My initial reaction is to say I generally oppose any effort to privatize public education. I believe that public schools should be open and accessible to all children, and they should be accountable to the public. When private operators start running schools with public funds, it becomes more difficult to guarantee the rights of students, parents, and teachers. However, you've raised several issues about privatization that are rarely considered, and I am open to discussing these.

As we know, teachers' unions have been the most vocal in their criticisms of privatization efforts, and I generally agree with them. We have several examples of teachers at for-profit schools being fired because they object to working long hours, and they have no union protection as a recourse.[2] If we want talented people to become teachers, and if we want them to stay in the profession, we have to make sure that they are treated with dignity and are paid adequately. Unions are better at ensuring this, and I think you and I both know that a primary motive for pursuing privatization is to undermine teachers' unions. It's also one of the reasons why I support teacher tenure. If teachers don't have job security, it will be even harder to attract talented people into the profession.

I'm also concerned about privatization because we've seen that when other public services are privatized, there is typically little incentive to ensure equitable access or to maintain quality. I'm thinking of cities that have privatized the operation of museums, parks, or other public services. Privately operated prisons are particularly notorious for the abuse and exploitation of inmates. I worry that the privatization of education will go the same route. Already, we have many examples of children being counseled out of for-profit schools because they are deemed hard to serve.[3]

However, you correctly point out that we have lived with various forms of public-private partnerships for years in education: in construction, in the use of headhunters to recruit top administrators, and in the provision of a variety of services that schools need. Additionally, many families sue public school districts because they fail to adequately serve the needs of learning-disabled students. When they win, they are able to get districts to pay for their children to attend privately operated schools, often at great expense to taxpayers. I support the rights of parents to do this.

So I think we should try to look at the issue on a pragmatic and less ideological basis: Under what conditions might a partnership with a private supplier of service be better than maintaining public control, and how should the use of public funds by private suppliers be monitored? I think posing the issue this way makes it possible to see the consequences of particular decisions.

Let's take up one of the examples you cited: Teach For America. I have mixed feelings about TFA. On the one hand, many of my students have joined the corps, and nearly all did so because they wanted to serve in disadvantaged public schools. Some have gone on to have long, distinguished careers in education.

However, to me, it makes little sense to place smart college grads with relatively little training into hard-to-staff schools serving needy kids. These kids need highly skilled teachers, not beginners. Affluent public schools and even many KIPP schools don't take TFA novices. In many cases, KIPP will make them work for a year as a teaching associate before placing them in a classroom.

Unfortunately, some public schools have come to rely on these inexperienced teachers because they have trouble recruiting others. Not long ago, I was told by the director of TFA in New Mexico that if it weren't for TFA, there wouldn't be enough teachers to staff schools on the reservations. I pointed out that this was an inadequate solution because TFAers rarely stay long enough to get good at teaching. To me, the only way to address the teacher shortage on the reservations is to train Native American kids to become teachers so that they can serve their people. Building a pipeline into the teaching profession may take time, but it's far more promising than the constant turnover that is reinforced when schools rely upon TFA.

Let's take up another example you raised: On the question of for-profit charter schools, I think the number of cases where public funds have been misused and children have been shortchanged are so great that there's good reason to oppose the practice altogether. However, I also know of private companies that are contracted by school districts to run schools or provide services to schools for kids that public schools often have a poor track record with, namely, formerly incarcerated youth, kids in foster care, and so on, and that do a much better job than traditional public schools. So I am not dismissive of the idea entirely.

What are your thoughts?—Pedro

Dear Pedro,

I thoroughly appreciate your thoughtful, measured take. Especially given how hot the emotions run on this topic, it's a welcome departure. First off, just to make sure we're not talking past each other, I agree that there's nothing magical about the private sector. Although for-profits have attributes that make them a healthy part of the educational ecosystem, that doesn't mean that for-profit providers are "better" than public or nonprofit ones. It's more useful to say that they're *different*, with distinctive strengths and weaknesses.

Traditional school systems involve public employees spending public funds to provide a service in accord with the directives of elected officials. This permits voters to hold policymakers accountable for the results. The downside: Elected officials have a lot of temptation to micromanage and to promote their particular agendas, yielding red tape and interference. They also tend to be responsive to politically powerful, vocal interests, all of which can lead to prioritizing those interests over student needs, cost-effective operations, or learning outcomes.

Nonprofits are independent and generate revenue by contracting with public agencies or raising money from donors. Their autonomy rests on the inclinations of whoever is cutting the checks to underwrite their work. This means they need to be closely attuned to shifts in foundation strategy and public policy. That can carry steep costs, leaving them susceptible to chasing fads and to the shifting winds of public opinion.

The logic of for-profits, of course, is a little different still. Because they need to make a profit, they have a fierce incentive to focus on maximizing revenue and minimizing costs. Thus, they wind up behaving quite differently than they would if they were overseen by elected officials or had to worry about philanthropic agendas.

None of these approaches is inherently "better" than the others. Each has weaknesses. And although there are certainly traditional public districts that do a terrific job of meeting a vast array of student needs, not every district clears that bar. As you note in the case of remediation, it's not hard to see how specialized, focused nonprofit or for-profit providers can sometimes help. It's the same as when the Environmental Protection Agency or a municipal public transit provider uses for-profit subcontractors to help fulfill their public mission.

You ask when I think private provision might be preferable to public. It comes down to their relative strengths. Public providers are designed to balance competing demands and needs, whereas I think for-profits are frequently better at executing a clearly articulated mission. This means that for-profits may be especially well suited for discrete, measurable tasks—like operating tutoring, self-contained programs, or schools with a distinct purpose. Of course, as you suggest, the self-interested nature of for-profits means that they should be closely monitored with clear metrics regarding cost, transparency, and performance.

That said, I'll try to address some of the specific concerns you raise. You observe that nonpublic providers, like TFA, often provide imperfect solutions to public problems. That's certainly true. But the thing is, the public system hasn't done much to solve the problem in question and doesn't seem to have a clear idea on how it should do so. Given that, I have trouble seeing how folks take issue with TFA for providing a private and temporary solution where public policy and publicly subsidized teacher training programs have failed to provide any solution at all.

You suggest that for-profit providers have no incentive to ensure equitable access and that they frequently counsel out disadvantaged students. I hear you, but think this is far too sweeping a stance. This isn't a simple public versus private issue. There are public magnet schools, public performing arts schools, and public exam schools that select their students, often screening out the most disadvantaged kids along the way. And we've both expressed concerns with how traditional districts treat these students. The issue of equitable access is a real one, but it applies to much more than for-profits. Meanwhile, when low-income students are given access to well-funded choice programs and provider performance is effectively monitored, I'd argue that for-profits have selfish cause to responsibly serve those who've long been left behind. It's all about making sure the incentives are aligned with what we want for-profits to do.

Finally, you suggest that for-profit schools take advantage of teachers by making them work long hours or treating them capriciously. Although I don't want to dismiss your concern, I see things a little differently. Generally speaking, I don't believe that anyone has systematic data on the hours worked or teacher grievances in for-profit schools. So any discussion is necessarily anecdotal. And you're obviously right that there have been complaints, just as there are about nonprofit and traditional district schools. These concerns should be treated seriously. At the same time, three-fourths of teachers in traditional schools say they want unions to make it simpler to remove ineffective teachers, pointing to their concerns that it's too hard to remove colleagues who aren't shouldering their share of the load.[4] And, without excusing genuine misconduct, part of the issue may be that for-profits or charter schools are striking a more rigorous balance than traditional public systems.

More generally, I'm unconvinced that "public" status necessarily promotes professionalism when it comes to equitable access, ensuring quality, or worker pay. I'd argue that government-employed attorneys, physicians, and pilots earn less and frequently feel less valued than their private-sector counterparts. Indeed, we've noted before that there are plenty of school systems where public control has yielded inequitable treatment and dismal quality.

There's much that can be said for public provision and traditional school districts. No argument. At the same time, I believe that nonprofit and for-profit providers both have a part to play in meeting the diverse needs of tens of millions of students and families.

Best,
Rick

Dear Rick,

Thanks for the thoughtful response to my last letter. I appreciate your willingness to carefully weigh the pros and cons of private versus public providers of services. Having served on the school board in

Berkeley, California, I understand all too well the need for efficiently and responsibly using public funds, especially during a period of austerity.

However, I want to return to a more basic principle: the importance of "public" in public education. The whole idea of public schools, like public parks and public transportation, is under attack. Trump has referred to them as "government" schools as a way of diminishing their importance and attacking their mission. Throughout our society, private goods and services are generally seen as superior to those that are available to the public. It would be a shame if this is how we come to see public schools.

As we know, public services, whether they be for health, transportation, air travel, or education, are essential to a democratic society. When all of us rely on public services like these, we become invested in ensuring that quality is maintained. However, in many cases, poor people rely more heavily on public services. For example, public buses generally serve more low-income than affluent people because poor people are less likely to own cars. In many areas, bus service is irregular and conditions on buses are often substandard. I don't believe this would occur if the affluent used public buses. Over and over we observe that when the broad public is less committed to supporting its public institutions and services, there is a strong tendency to allow them to deteriorate. But when we share and rely equally upon public goods, it binds us together in a good way.

If you don't mind, I'd like to raise a bit of history to support my argument. Frederick Law Olmsted, the architect who designed New York's Central Park and many others, understood that shared public spaces were important in a society characterized by class hierarchy. When rich and poor are compelled to share public space, it is easier to recognize our common humanity. New Yorkers see this on the subways where over four million people a day rely on the nation's largest transportation system. Having been raised in New York, I often marveled at seeing men (usually White) dressed in business suits, heading down to Wall Street, standing shoulder to shoulder with Black and Latino people from Harlem and the outer boroughs. Despite our differences, we share the need for safe, affordable, and reliable transportation. Regardless of who you are or where you enter, you pay the same fare and are subject to the same conditions—oppressive heat in the summer, freezing cold in the winter, and rats year-round. The system works (even when the subways run late) because everyone uses it and there's really no alternative.

Public schools should work in the same way. However, as inequality and race or class segregation in society have increased, our public schools have reflected these trends, as wealthy and more advantaged families retreated into private schools.[5] As a result, in many cities we've seen a steady disinvestment in public schools, not because the remaining students need less, but because the families they serve are less politically empowered. And disinvestment is only part of the problem: The poor remaining in these schools are unable to build social networks with students from other backgrounds, and wealthier students don't have as many opportunities to learn to empathize with the experiences of others.

I believe that public education is a precious resource that is still the foundation of American democracy, but it's in trouble and needs to be defended.—Pedro

---

Dear Pedro,

Your Olmsted example hits home. I absolutely take the point on the democratizing nature of New York City's subway system—same fare, same oppressive heat, same freezing cold for everyone. I agree that there's something hugely healthy about that. And I also think you're right about the value of children seeing adults of all backgrounds, professional roles, and races interacting as compatriots. Especially in our polarized era, it'd be a mistake to underestimate how that kind of shared experience can help bind communities together.

Where we see the issue of "publicness" differently, I think, is in whether we should pursue our shared goals via uniform, publicly operated infrastructure. Whatever its flaws, New York City's subway truly is a marvel. But there are only a handful of cities with similarly expansive, ubiquitous subway systems. In the rest of the nation, including in most big cities, there is just too much sprawl, too little density, and too many impediments for subways to play the same role. That isn't a knock on New York's system, Boston's T, or Chicago's L, it's just to note that what works in a handful of compact cities isn't the answer in many other places. I think this can be a useful frame for thinking about schooling.

Like cities, students are different, and I'm skeptical that there's a particular pedagogy or approach that will work for every child. This is part of what makes schooling wildly challenging work. It's doubly so when it comes to struggling learners beset by poverty, unstable homes, and unsafe environs. The work is so hard that we need to use all the tools at our disposal.

I lean toward a broader, more expansive notion of what constitutes "public." To use a different illustration, recall that taxis were once regarded as "public" cars because they were shared by many users. When I see municipalities welcome bike-share programs, dedicated biking lanes, electric scooters, Zipcar, rideshare options, and more, the mix of public oversight, public services, nonprofit activity, and for-profit operations looks to me like a tapestry of public provision. This is, obviously, quite different from the subway experience you describe but it has other virtues: among them, customization, cost effectiveness, and convenience. And, in many places, it may just be a more dynamic, practical solution for transportation. The same applies for schooling.

The bottom line is that the "publicness" of public schooling is more complicated than we often acknowledge. There are admired public schools that have admissions criteria (like New York City's famed magnets). There are public systems that charge families when students play sports or use musical equipment. Some public school systems rely on private contractors to serve students with special needs or to provide needed services. None of this necessarily means these schools and systems are no longer public. It does mean that the whole idea of public is less straightforward than our debates tend to suggest.

So here's where I think we stand in terms of common ground. We generally agree that the debates about the value of public versus private ought to be more pragmatic and less ideological. Overheated attacks on "government schools" don't help clarify things; neither do jeremiads skewering nonprofits as "privatizers" or for-profits as evil incarnate.

Given all of our good-faith differences here, I'm looking forward to your take.

Best,

Rick

Dear Rick,

This may be a place where we just have to agree to disagree. Although I think having a taxi or bicycle available at a charge to the public is a useful service, it's not the same as a guarantee that clear water will be available when you open the tap, or that the public school in your neighborhood will adequately serve your children's needs. You make valid points that some forms of privatization may be helpful, but I can't agree that having a mix of for-profit, nonprofit, and public schools provides the same guarantees with respect to access as a traditional public system.

I still believe that public education should be the glue that holds us together. Today, that's rarely the case, except in some rural and suburban communities where there are fewer "choices" or options available. I am particularly concerned now because, as a result of the pandemic, we're seeing many affluent people withdraw from public schools to create private "pods" consisting of small groups of kids that can cost as much as $30,000 a year.[6] What will happen to kids from low-income families who will have to rely on remote learning?

In New York, I can think of several public high schools that were once described as a "superhighway" to the middle class. Many of them don't work like that now. That's the way Arthur Levine, the former president at Teachers College, Columbia University, described his alma mater, DeWitt Clinton High School in the Bronx. Up until the 1960s, this massive school with over 5,000 students was racially integrated and sent lots of its graduates to college. The school has distinguished alumni that include actors (Burt Lancaster), writers (James Baldwin), generals, judges, and others. Today, DeWitt Clinton is a shell of its former self. With fewer than 3,000 students, it serves more homeless kids than any school in New York City and offers very few college prep courses.

I can think of other examples like this one that are emblematic of the decline in public support for public schools. Shortly after arriving to Los Angeles, I was asked to speak at City Hall to a group of civic leaders about education. At the start of my talk, I asked those assembled how many had attended public schools in Los Angeles. Nearly the entire room raised their hands. I then asked how many had children or grandchildren enrolled in Los Angeles public schools, and almost no one raised a hand. A similar pattern of middle-class flight (especially the White middle class) has occurred in urban school systems across the country, and it has contributed to the decline in support for public schools.

As I've said repeatedly throughout our exchange, we have ample evidence that when we concentrate the most disadvantaged kids in certain schools, we significantly increase the likelihood of failure.

I don't have an easy answer for how we reverse this trend, but I think we must, or our society is in trouble. The more divided our society becomes, the less we are able to address our challenges as a nation. I have little faith that further privatizing schools will bring us closer together or help kids in need.—Pedro

CHAPTER 9

Philanthropy

Big-dollar education philanthropy has become controversial, with supporters arguing that funders have helped to drive much-needed improvement, and skeptics arguing that wealthy elites are buying influence over public institutions. Pedro, though acknowledging the value of the work that many small foundations do, criticizes large philanthropies for their outsize role and for trampling public sentiment while advancing ineffective, unpopular policies. He is particularly troubled by the lack of transparent decisionmaking, public accountability, and reporting that has marked many big-dollar initiatives. Although Rick shares some of Pedro's concerns, he offers a more favorable take—suggesting that philanthropy can serve as a "healthy check on the inertia, interest group politics, and bureaucratic routines that so often characterize public governance." Indeed, Rick sees philanthropy playing an invaluable role in producing a more pluralistic, responsive, and "democratic" education system—so long as the community of donors is cultivating competing visions and rejecting the temptations of groupthink. Despite their differences on this topic, Rick and Pedro close with firm agreement regarding the need for transparency and the public reporting of results. Key questions include whether foundations are antidemocratic or a part of a healthy pluralism, what it means for funders to be transparent and accountable, and what role philanthropy should ultimately play in schooling.

Dear Rick,

Let's talk about the role private philanthropies play in shaping education policy. On the one hand, philanthropies do many things that are clearly quite beneficial. Some that I have worked with fund libraries, art, and music, and donate money to get books into schools. Others focus on expanding access to preschool and after-school programs, and some specialize in helping the most at-risk children, such as those in foster care.

However, the good work that many have done has been over-shadowed by the fact that in recent years, a small number of large foundations, namely Gates, Broad, and Walton, have played an out-size role in shaping the direction of education policy. With their abil-ity to make large donations to politicians and civic organizations, these foundations have exerted enormous influence. Their interven-tions behind the scenes have generated criticism from both the Left and Right because of the way in which they undermine the demo-cratic process.

For example, during the Obama administration, the Gates Founda-tion was extremely influential in developing the Common Core stan-dards. Working with David Coleman, before he became president of the College Board, and Gene Wilhoit, director of a national group of state school chiefs, the foundation gave out lots of money to groups on the Left and the Right to win support for the Common Core. They argued that the new standards would boost achievement and create greater equity among the states by ensuring that all kids were exposed to high academic standards. With Gates's money and the federal gov-ernment's willingness to use Race to the Top funds as leverage, within just 2 years, 45 states and the District of Columbia adopted the Common Core.

Now to be clear, my issue is with the lack of transparency and ac-countability in the foundations' actions and not the Common Core it-self. I never opposed the Common Core. In fact, I think standards are essential for equity, and make sense. As you know, the standards don't dictate what kids learn; they are simply designed to ensure that there is some consistency in what kids are exposed to during their education. In school districts where the Common Core was implemented well, I have heard from teachers that it has had a positive effect on learning.

However, I find the means through which the foundation exerted its influence quite troubling. Instead of public hearings over the Common Core, the standards were rammed through, often without even a vote of the state legislature. As a result, rather than an open hearing that might have allowed some helpful modifications to be considered, the standards were adopted without much thought about impact. In some states, such as New York and Delaware, the standardized tests based on the Common Core standards were implemented before teachers were trained on how to teach them. This led to a huge anti-testing backlash among parents who rightfully objected to the way the tests and standards were being used.

I recognize that democracy is often messy, but when we allow those with wealth and power to impose their will on the rest of us, we lose.

One reason we lose out is that the foundations don't always think through their investments and are quick to move on before solving the problem they once were interested in. I'm sure you remember that a while back, the Gates Foundation was enamored with the idea of creating small schools. Over the course of several years, the foundation gave over $2 billion to school districts throughout the country for the purpose of converting large, comprehensive high schools into smaller ones.[1] The idea seemed reasonable because large high schools had been criticized for being impersonal and alienating. In urban areas, many were also unsafe and academically weak. However, as you and I both know, it takes more than being small to create a great or even good school. The Gates Foundation ignored the need for a strategy to improve teaching and learning, to improve school culture, and to bring in the social supports that schools serving poor children need (e.g., social workers, health care, after-school programs, etc.).

I think that if the foundation had developed its plans in the open and in consultation with educators, they would have realized it takes more than shrinking a school to help it improve. There are, after all, lots of small schools that are awful. Instead, as it became clear that the movement for small schools was not producing the sweeping changes they had hoped for, they simply aborted the experiment and moved on to yet another set of reforms.

Another reason we lose when philanthropies impose their will is that they often push policies that compromise the quality of public education. This idea seems to have been lost on our current secretary of education, Betsy DeVos. Although she did not lead one of the big foundations, her family foundation played a major role in promoting choice and vouchers in Michigan. Anyone who has visited schools in Flint or Detroit, public or charter, can observe firsthand the devastating consequences of this experimentation. In Detroit, the schools are literally falling apart despite the promise that "choice" would lead to renewal.

Fortunately, sometimes those with vast sums of money don't prevail. We saw this with Mike Bloomberg's presidential campaign. Despite spending over one billion of his own money on his 4-month campaign, more than Obama spent in 2012, Bloomberg failed to gain traction with voters.[2] Similarly, Eli Broad poured money into school board races in Los Angeles, and at one point called for half of the schools in Los Angeles to become charter schools.[3] This led to a huge backlash by the teachers union, which regarded the proliferation of charter schools as an existential threat. So I don't mean to imply that philanthropists are all-powerful.

That said, although I think that many schools can benefit from philanthropy, there are huge problems when their influence dictates the direction of policy. What do you think, Rick?—Pedro

---

Dear Pedro,

Whew! You've got us off to a roaring start on this one.

I'll begin with what I read as your biggest concern: the antidemocratic nature of big philanthropy. I hear you and think you raise real issues. But though I too have reservations, I'm generally supportive of the role played by big donors.

Much of the time, I think philanthropy helps make for a *more* pluralistic, responsive education system by supporting voices, programs, and organizations that challenge the routines of district and state machinery. Philanthropy can provide a foothold to those who are otherwise boxed out by teachers' unions, education bureaucracies, textbook companies, and education schools. It enables outsiders to make the case for alternative policies and to launch promising ventures.

More generally, I see the world as invariably filled with people who have a grossly outsize ability to shape public policy. When I look at the talking heads on CNN, FOX, or MSNBC, I see plenty of lapdogs and ideologues with what feels like a disturbingly large impact on the public square. Big-shot athletes, actors, and CEOs have platforms to influence public affairs that can bear little relation to their expertise or wisdom. But the ability of all these figures to speak and shape public policy is part of the fabric of freedom. Even when I find their contributions misguided, I believe the risks of regulating or restricting their influence would dwarf any potential benefits. I think the same logic applies when it comes to donors who deal in dollars rather than followers.

That said, I think philanthropy's value ultimately rests on how philanthropists approach their role. When donors promote a rich array of views, values, and approaches, philanthropy is enormously valuable. When they start singing from the same hymnal and throwing their weight around in ways that shrink the range of permissible perspectives, programs, and policies, that's a different story. From the frenzied enthusiasm for test-based teacher evaluation to the more recent push for "antiracist" education, I've too often found groupthink to be the norm.

My big concern is how human nature makes it easy for funders to adopt the kind of insular groupthink that, as you note, marked Gates's "small schools" push. The fact is that foundation staff are treated with kid gloves. They spend every day talking about their vision and mission, mostly with people who have their money or want their money. It's easy for them to wind up in a self-assured, mission-driven bubble.

From inside that bubble, almost any criticism can seem misinformed or unfair and is often taken as proof that the critic "just doesn't get it." That can undermine healthy discussion. That's doubly true when big foundations collaborate, supersizing the resources behind a given push and leaving those with questions or concerns to feel like they're being shut out and trampled.

This dynamic played a big role in the travails of the Common Core. Whatever its merits, I agree with you that the Common Core was ultimately undone by the maneuverings of its *supporters*. The energetic backing of big funders and federal officials denied the Common Core the chance to grow organically. Parents and teachers never got much chance to kick its tires, raise qualms, or seek modifications. Instead, due largely to the full-court press engineered by enthusiastic foundation staff, the standards seemed to drop fully formed onto states and then into millions of classrooms. This dynamic gave rise to endless concerns about everything from ludicrous math assignments to a war on fiction. But advocates and funders were already so invested that they found it tough to course correct or even take the problems seriously.

I'll close by pointing to a concern that we share, which is the maddening fact that funders and foundation staff seem so profoundly unaccountable. After all, during the past decade or two, funders have talked a lot about the importance of holding schools and educators accountable. And yet, when foundation agendas disappoint or even wreak havoc, it's all too easy for staff to just brush their hands and blithely move on to the next big thing. Now, I'm not interested in formal public accountability for private giving, but I'd love to see an ethos in which foundations and their employees took more ownership for the consequences of their handiwork.

Although we may disagree as to whether big philanthropy is good or bad for schooling, I suspect we may still find a good bit of common ground on the risks of groupthink and the question of accountability. I'll look forward to your thoughts.

Best,

Rick

Dear Rick,

Let's start with where we have common ground. It would be hypocritical of me to criticize the big foundations too harshly because I am familiar with some of the good work all of the major ones do. I have also received funding from Gates to study schools for boys, and from Broad to study the education and development of Black children in Los Angeles. I appreciate the support I have received for this research, and like others in academia who rely on foundations to support research that draws attentions to the flaws of education policy, I know that if we are too dependent on government funding (federal or state), some of our independence would be compromised.

I also know that private foundations frequently fund innovative schools and practices that might otherwise never have seen the light of day. For example, some of the best work in community schools—those schools like the Harlem Children's Zone, that offer a full range of health and social services, as well as high-quality preschool, after-school, and summer school to poor kids—would not have been possible without the support of private foundations. In Oklahoma, partnerships between local school districts and private foundations have made it possible for that state to become the leader in making high-quality preschool available to large numbers of children. The foundations deserve credit for funding this work.

So, like you, I think that we must be balanced in our criticisms. But, as you note, there is plenty worth criticizing. Beyond their overreach on the Common Core, teacher evaluation, and charter schools (although we may disagree on the latter), I am particularly critical of their unwillingness to evaluate their priorities and projects. This is related to the lack of accountability you mentioned in your last letter. Many foundations embrace a focus area for a while—reading programs, girls' education, youth development, and so on—and then shift gears without ever explaining what they learned or what impact their funding has had. Generally, the shift occurs not because they solved the problem that they once regarded as important, but usually because they have adopted new priorities.

For example, if the Gates Foundation had offered a thorough, public critique of what it learned from the money it invested in the effort to convert some large schools into smaller ones, I think the field of education would have benefited. Several researchers (myself included) did their own evaluation of the initiative, but having worked in New York during the Bloomberg years when a lot of money was spent on creating small schools, I know that some were great and some were not. We need to understand what factors made it possible for some of the new schools to be successful. We also need to know whether this reform had any ancillary benefits to other schools, or conversely, whether it made the challenges they face worse (there's some evidence that it did). Such transparency is critical if we are to avoid repeating the mistakes of the past.

Finally, I'd like to return to the undemocratic tendencies among the big foundations that concern me and many others. In an interview describing his new book, *Just Giving: Why Philanthropy Is Failing America and How It Can Do Better*, Stanford professor Rob Reich argues that "Big Philanthropy is definitionally a plutocratic voice in our democracy, an exercise of power by the wealthy that is unaccountable, non-transparent, donor-directed, perpetual, and tax-subsidized."[4] He points out that wealthy individuals who donate to foundations are often able to direct funding to their pet causes instead of paying taxes. In a society where inequality is already extreme and wealthy individuals exercise enormous control over politics and the economy, I believe the growing influence of private foundations in education that we both agree are often unaccountable poses a serious threat to our future. For public education to fulfill its mission of preparing students to participate in democracy, schools must be accountable to the public, not a handful of wealthy individuals.—Pedro

---

Dear Pedro,

I respect Rob Reich, appreciate his scholarship, and enjoy his company. I consider him a friend. Even so, I can't help but chuckle when I hear a tenured Stanford professor lament that someone else enjoys unaccountable, opaque, tax-subsidized influence in the public square.

I don't mean to sound flippant or to pooh-pooh the larger point that you and Reich raise. Over the years, I've written at length about the various problems with big funders, including the cavalier cycling of agendas and lack of accountability that you flag.[5] So I'm not trying to make the case that donors are necessarily noble, wise, or deserving of flower-strewn parades.

Nonetheless, while Reich is concerned that philanthropic K–12 spending puts a plutocratic thumb on the scale, I'm more concerned that a lack of private activity removes a healthy check on the inertia, interest group politics, and bureaucratic routines that so often characterize public governance. Indeed, given that *all* K–12 philanthropy combined amounts to less than one percent of what taxpayers spend on public schooling each year, I find the notion that schools will be more accountable to a handful of wealthy individuals than to "the public" an unhelpful caricature.

For one thing, there's more to "the public" than just elected government officials: "Public" oversight also encompasses parents who can vote with their feet, journalists who can expose wrongdoing, and researchers who can highlight a school's successes and shortcomings. And all of these have benefited significantly from funder support. For another, practically speaking, even when I've fumed at major funders, I think it's rare that their impact has superseded the influence of unions, trade groups, professional associations, and partisan activists. Whatever reservations I have about philanthropy, I don't believe that reducing its role would yield more farsighted, responsible, or carefully wrought policies and practices. Instead, I suspect it would mostly empower ambitious politicos, powerful interest groups, and those academics and advocates who possess big megaphones.

And, though your point about the influence of the wealthy is well taken, I'd find such concerns more compelling if that moral outrage were consistently applied. Many of those who worry about the baleful influence of big-dollar giving seem to suddenly find it okay, even laudable, when they like the cause. You talked a few letters back about the self-financed 2020 presidential campaign by billionaire and former New York City mayor Mike Bloomberg. After Bloomberg's campaign tanked, impassioned progressives penned a sheaf of columns explaining that he could buy his way back into their good graces by spending big to register Democratic voters and support Democratic candidates.

Indeed, many of the same voices that denounce deep-pocketed backers of school choice seem unperturbed—or even enthusiastic—when billionaires like Bloomberg or George Soros give vast sums to promote gun control or some other favored cause. Rather than selectively (and oft hypocritically) decrying this giving, I think we might do better to recognize it as an intrinsic part of our pluralistic tradition, whether or not we agree with the agenda at work.

So, although philanthropy certainly has its share of problems, I'd argue that a vibrant philanthropic sector is far better than the alternative. How's that for an inspired defense?

Best,

Rick

Dear Rick,

Well, your last letter got me a bit defensive when you took swipes at professors. I think there's lots of room for critique of those of us who make our living in the ivory tower, but I don't think that accusing us of undue influence in policy is fair or accurate. I know that you produce the education scholar rankings each year, so you have a keen sense of who in academia is influential and who is not.[6] However, even those who are consistently at the top of the list pale in comparison to the big private foundations when it comes to exerting influence over public policy.

Of course, this is because the foundations have deep pockets. Money can move policy and as we know, it can influence elections, too. In fact, I think our democracy is threatened by the tremendous influence that individuals with wealth exert over the political process. For example, while the current secretary of education, Betsy DeVos, was involved with education in Michigan, largely as a philanthropist who gave money to charter schools, do you think she was appointed because of her knowledge or experience in education? I think not. I say this not simply because I disagree with her politics or policies (remember, I was also publicly critical of Arne Duncan and the Obama administration), but because I think she was appointed since she and her family are very rich. I don't think this is how democracy or our government should work.

If it were up to me, education would be a nonpartisan issue, not a bipartisan one. Politicians should not be able to tamper with schools or education policy any more than they should be allowed to tamper with our roads, the water supply, or utilities. Uh oh, I forgot; they tamper with these public services, too. Perhaps that's the reason why our infrastructure is in such bad shape now. I think we're in trouble, Rick.

Again, I don't think the foundations and big philanthropy are the enemies; however, I do think we should all be concerned about the excessive influence exerted by a few wealthy individuals. Our future is at stake and I'm concerned about it. How about you?—Pedro

---

Dear Pedro,

I absolutely hear you about the problems with the rich throwing their weight around. I get it. And yet, on this one, we come out in pretty different places. After reflecting on our back-and-forth, I'll try to offer a few thoughts as to why.

At the end of the day, I think we've got an honest disagreement as to whether philanthropy's role as a check on other institutions is outweighed by the tremendous influence it can give to donors. For me, philanthropy can be a useful check on entrenched interests, surfacing competing ideas and supporting those with the will to challenge the way things are.

Would those concerned about the influence of private philanthropy really want to get rid of what it's made possible? Critics would have a hard time convincing me that we'd be better off if donors had never helped give rise to *Sesame Street*, the National Assessment of Educational

Progress, charter schooling, the Harlem Children's Zone, or the push for social-emotional learning. And if their assumption is that, absent philanthropy, government would have done all of these things anyway, I'd suggest they need to think again.

In any event, it occurs to me that what may have gotten lost in this discussion is the reality that large-scale donors account for only a limited slice of total philanthropy.[7] The United States has tens of thousands of (mostly small, mostly local) donors, and yet the attention paid to philanthropy tends to concentrate on the same half dozen or so. It's striking, because I've been in a number of conversations where an educator or academic lamented big-donor influence and then, in the next breath, spoke of the wonderful program that they launched . . . with support from a small local donor. Education philanthropy is a complex sector and a big chunk of it is local, modest, and pedestrian. As we try to make sense of it, we should take care that our understandable interest in billionaire heavyweights doesn't obscure this reality.

I do want to touch upon one other point you raised earlier, one where we wholly agree. Funders should aggressively study their efforts, welcome tough-minded evaluations, and be both candid and public about the results. After all, my support for philanthropy rests, in large part, on the conviction that an array of competing approaches can yield new insights, advance public understanding, and challenge convenient conventions. If foundations don't invest in careful scrutiny of their work and in sharing the results, much of this gets lost.

Although there needs to be much more ambitious evaluation, it's a mistake to suggest that it never occurs. Whatever my concerns about the Gates Foundation, for instance, it was admirably transparent in its support for RAND Corporation's extensive evaluation of its massive Effective Teacher Initiative. RAND ultimately deemed the $575 million, 7-year effort a failure, pretty much putting a fork in that work.[8] But we learned a great deal along the way about how strategies to evaluate teachers and boost teacher quality played out in practice. We need much more of that kind of work. We also need to acknowledge it when we see it.

A final thought, for what it's worth. For all my reservations about philanthropy, I'd rather have wealthy people supporting education than buying additional homes and fancy cars. Even when I disagree with what a particular donor is doing, I can appreciate the act of giving. And it seems to me that a major complaint about big philan-thropy, for many critics, is less about the giving and more about the fact that the superwealthy are so rich in the first place.

At that point, we're no longer really talking about education or phi-lanthropy. We're into a more fundamental debate about property, taxes, liberty, and equality. When we've come to this point, it suggests that we've reached the end of this trail and that it's time to turn the page.

Best,
Rick

CHAPTER 10

Diversity and Equity

Issues of diversity and equity are at the center of contemporary efforts to improve schooling. During Rick and Pedro's correspondence, this topic was pushed to the forefront of the national consciousness by massive protests against police brutality and calls for a national reckoning on race. In this chapter, Rick and Pedro concur that schools must find ways to nurture, support, and instruct a student population that's changed dramatically over time. Pedro goes further, stressing that meaningful progress on equity and inclusion requires measures to address systemic racism. He calls for increased diversity in the teaching workforce, an end to the "'whitewashing' of the curriculum," and more mentorship and support for students of color, while suggesting that "such measures can be implemented without alienating White children or their parents." Rick evinces sympathy for several of Pedro's specific recommendations but is troubled that supporting this agenda means giving a pass to champions of diversity and equity who seem intent on promoting ideological orthodoxy and spreading "troubling" new racial doctrines. Major themes in this chapter include how schools should respond to an increasingly diverse student population, what it means for educators to respect the needs and cultures of all their students, and whether "antiracist" efforts can themselves become an exercise in hate and oppression.

Dear Rick,

Over 65 years after the *Brown v. Board of Education* decision, many kids in America are still attending schools that are segregated on the basis of race and class. Of course, this is not legally enforced segregation, but segregation maintained by the way we organize schools and set district boundaries. Today, the average Black student is most likely to attend a school where 49% of the students are Black. For Latino students, the patterns are even more extreme. Fifty-seven percent of Latino students attend schools where the majority of students are Latino.[1]

These averages fail to capture the hypersegregation by race and class common in most urban schools throughout the United States. Black and Latino students in the United States are most likely to attend schools where the majority of children are poor and the resources available to serve them are inadequate.[2] This is the case in poor, predominantly Black cities like Baltimore, Newark, and Detroit; and it is also true in integrated, prosperous cities like San Francisco, New York, and Los Angeles. The evidence is clear: Not only have we failed to live up to the promise of *Brown v. Board of Education,* we have failed to even deliver on the promise of *Plessy v. Ferguson*: separate but equal.

Furthermore, in another sign of retreat away from our nation's commitment to integration, several communities that once had relatively integrated schools have either opted out of public education altogether for private schools or found ways to secede from districts entirely by creating separate, racially homogenous schools and districts where the majority of students are White and affluent.[3] As I mentioned in the Achievement Gap letters, the number of schools in which less than 10% of students are White has more than tripled in the last 25 years for which we have data.[4]

Ironically, the resegregation of American schools is occurring at a time when the nation is becoming significantly more diverse. Recent reports from the census show that just under 50% of children under the age of 15 in America are White.[5] Much of the change can be attributed to the growth of the Latino and Asian populations.

And many predominantly White communities may not realize that schools have become more segregated. As the percentage of White students in U.S. schools has declined, so too has the degree and likelihood of White isolation. About one in five White students attend a school with 10% or fewer children of color.[6] Nationally, the typical White student is now in a school where the student composition is nearly three-fourths White, one-eighth Latino, and one-twelfth Black.

Although many affluent children of color also attend racially diverse schools, most children of color experience what might be termed "double segregation": separation by race and class. As we've previously discussed, increased racial isolation is typically accompanied by concentrating the poorest and most disadvantaged students in urban and some rural schools. Remarkably, segregation is no longer acknowledged by policymakers as an obstacle to educational advancement, and neither is poverty, though it is apparent that both factors continue to be major obstacles to progress.

The majority of kids who have been left behind educationally and economically are racial minorities. However, there are also plenty of White children who find themselves in this situation, too, but White poverty is pretty much invisible in America. I spoke to principals in Vermont a few years ago and I was surprised to learn that the big equity issue they wanted to talk about was the opioid crisis. This is a state that is 93% White and has a poverty rate of 11%.[7] However, I learned that most high school graduates in Vermont don't go to college, and those who can find it necessary to leave the state in search of jobs elsewhere. Principals told me about kids who go through the winter without heat in their houses. One principal told me that he had just found out that 30 of his students had been placed in foster care because their parents had been arrested during drug raids.

Although addiction doesn't discriminate, the ability to get treatment and to recover economically and socially does. The crisis ravaged the poorest communities, especially White communities in rural areas.

I share this because the color of poverty and suffering in America is usually portrayed as Black, and occasionally Latino or Native American. Do you think that if more wealthy Americans knew that there were White kids who didn't have enough food to eat and were enrolled in underresourced schools, they would be more sympathetic? I wonder.

In American education, we spend a lot of time debating diversity, equity, and inclusion, but so little addressing the structural inequities that pervade our society. Since the police murder of George Floyd in Minneapolis, these issues are getting more attention, but who knows if it will be sustained. We rely on education to promote social mobility across generations, but the evidence shows that this is becoming increasingly rare. Several studies have shown that kids who are born poor end up poor as adults.[8] The American dream is in serious trouble.

What do you think it will take to get Americans to see that, like it or not, the country is becoming more racially diverse, and if we don't ensure that all kids receive a good education, our future is in jeopardy?—Pedro

Dear Pedro,

It's good to hear from you, my friend. I like a lot of what you have to say here and appreciate the tenor of your note. When diversity and equity are framed as trying to better serve an increasingly diverse student population and equip all students to thrive, I'm all in. That's vital, essential work.

Every child deserves the opportunity to master essential skills, understand their world, develop their gifts, prepare for the responsibilities of citizenship, and pursue their dreams. For far too many children, as you make clear, this is manifestly not the case today. My experience is that most on the Left and the Right agree that we need to do better but have their own thoughts on how to make that happen.

That said, the notion that, generally speaking, White people don't care about the well-being of non-Whites is, I think, misguided and unsupported by evidence. And in my own experience, I've too often found proposals offered in the name of diversity and equity to be ideological and partisan, with the language of social justice a convenient cloak for ideas I regard as profoundly problematic and a poor basis for a successful, harmonious, multiracial society.

But we agree that action is required, even if we disagree about just what that should entail. Although I frequently hear it suggested that conservatives are bereft of ideas on this count, I flatly disagree. My friends on the Left may find fault with our prescriptions. But we've certainly got them. School choice can help free kids stuck in stagnant schools. Expanded career and technical education and licensure reform can provide the skills and smash the paper barriers that have locked too many out of good jobs. Reforming land-use restrictions and zoning would make affordable housing more widely available and stop policy from encouraging residential stratification. Though there are certainly reasonable critiques of each of these ideas (just as conservatives can mount such critiques of progressive proposals), I think we can find common ground in agreeing that there's much that needs to be done.

With that, I'd like to turn to a question that loomed large for me as I read your thoughtful letter: Given the seriousness of the practical challenges you sketch, why has so much of the ensuing discussion been dominated by those whose real passion seems to be polarizing cultural agendas?

I welcome hard-hitting debates about how to improve quality and equity in early childhood, K–12, and higher education. But I'm honestly perplexed by why so many discussions of racial equity today seem to devolve into attacks on the intellectual and personal traits that equip students for personal and civic success.

For instance, the famed KIPP charter schools abandoned their longtime slogan of "Work Hard, Be Nice" after KIPP's leadership decided that the phrase hinders efforts to "dismantle systemic racism."[9] The National Museum of African American History and Culture featured a graphic on its website that described traits like "individualism," "hard work," "objectivity," "progress," "politeness," "decision-making," and "delayed gratification" as hallmarks of "White culture."[10] And the superintendent of New York's East Harlem Scholars Academies penned for *Education Week* a back-to-school missive instructing "White teachers" that they should steer away from "individual stories" of accomplishment, because doing so would "unintentionally teach students that 'really good, really successful' Black folks are exempt from racist structures."[11]

I find these cartoonish dogmas both insulting and insane. For one thing, I don't think anyone who's been to Singapore or South Korea would view traits like "hard work" or "politeness" as especially "White." For another, across Africa and South America, air traffic controllers and cardiovascular surgeons put a lot of faith in things like "decisionmaking" and "objectivity." And I can't help but think that we would rightly condemn as an anachronistic menace any good ol' boy who suggested that there was something uniquely "White" about being polite or working hard. So what are we to make of those who purport to be "antiracist" but promote the same cartoonish stereotypes?

Although I can work in good faith with those who disagree with me about pedagogy or policy, I can't with someone who expects me to condemn American history as little more than a "tale of racism and oppression" or who says that pointing out that $2 + 2 = 4$ "reeks of White supremacist patriarchy" or who insists that "Whiteness is a cancer." Yet, not only are such statements loudly and proudly shared under the banner of "antiracist" education, but they're frequently conjoined with disturbing assertions that those of us who disagree need to be reeducated into a more enlightened stance.

I want to be clear. It's not just the rhetoric that I find troubling, it's the substance. I believe the things these "antiracists" are preaching are harmful to our students, regardless of race. I find it appalling that teachers would hesitate to teach students to work hard or be kind. It's perverse to think teachers would shrink from celebrating iconic figures or individual accomplishment for fear of feeding into "racist structures." Indeed, it seems to me that "antiracism" is just a clever label for a new breed of rank bigotry.

And, it's infuriating because these evangelists of "antiracist" education are creating an unnecessary, impossible dilemma. While I want to work with you and so many others to expand opportunity and tackle real problems, I'm wholly unwilling to say or do things that will give a moral sanction to those working to sow divisive, destructive calumny in the name of "justice."

I'm left wondering how to reconcile your persuasive call to tackle undeniable social and economic needs with the reservations I have about so much of what I see traveling under the banner of equity and diversity.

Best,
Rick

Dear Rick,

Before weighing in on the controversy, I think we should restate the problem. The country has become substantially more racially and culturally diverse, and the students in our public schools reflect this trend, but the overwhelming majority of our teachers are White (almost 80%).[12] Today, over 50% of the public school population is composed of children who are not defined as "White."[13] But much of what children learn in school reflects the history and culture of the shrinking White majority.

Why is this a problem? Because most children of any race can't name a notable Asian or Latino figure in U.S. history. The same is true for African and Native Americans. Other than Martin Luther King, Jr., Harriet Tubman, and Pocahontas, most American children learn very little about the non-White people who have helped shape American history and culture. I believe the absence contributes to ignorance and pervasive racial bias.

However, the "whitewashing" of the curriculum isn't limited to so-cial studies and literature. For example, in math and science there is considerable evidence that people of color and women continue to be significantly underrepresented in STEM majors and professions.[14] Although the academic content in these subjects might appear to be race- and gender-neutral, without mentoring and active encourage-ment so that they see how their communities might benefit from the study of math and science, women and people of color often become discouraged from pursuing majors or careers in these fields.

When mentorship, support, and encouragement are provided, underrepresentation can be countered. For example, Freeman Hrabowski, who is president of the University of Maryland in Baltimore County (UMBC) and who happens to be a Black chemist, has an excellent track record of producing women and people of color with advanced degrees in STEM fields.[15] Similarly, little Xavier University in New Orleans, a historically Black Catholic college, produces more Black undergrads who are admitted to medical school each year than all of the Ivy League schools combined.[16]

People who have studied these issues point to the supportive cli-mate and culture at these schools, characteristics that are typically missing in most predominantly White universities. In such places, there not only tends to be a lack of mentoring that is critical for socializing a person into a new field, but there is often outright hostility to those who are different and presumed to not fit in.

If the teaching profession were more diverse, it is likely that we would not only see more women and people of color in STEM fields, but also improve academic performance and see fewer suspensions among children of color. This is confirmed by a recent study from Johns Hopkins, which drew upon longitudinal data from a national database.[17] The authors found that not only did the performance of Black students improve when they were taught by at least one Black teacher, but students of all races benefited.

There are, of course, significant obstacles that make increasing di-versity in the teaching profession difficult—low wages that make the teaching profession insufficiently attractive, a pipeline problem that results in too few college students of color choosing teaching as a field of study, poor working conditions, and so forth. However, this doesn't mean we couldn't take steps to address the problem. We could, for example, introduce young people to the teaching profession early by setting up pre-teacher academies in high schools.

Yet, even as we work on making the teaching profession more diverse, we also have to help the teachers we have now get better at serving our diverse student population. I say this not to blame teachers for patterns of low achievement among students of color; blame gets us nowhere and generally makes those we blame defensive. I believe that there are effective ways to help teachers get better at serving racial and ethnic minorities that don't have to make White teachers feel attacked.

For example, one of the things we can do is to learn from the schools where children of color are well served right now. Such schools show that we can improve academic outcomes for Black, Latino, and Native American students when we focus on the right things. This includes building strong relationships with kids of color, making the curriculum more culturally relevant and racially inclusive, engaging parents in partnerships rooted in trust and respect, and so on. By adopting these and other measures, we can create more schools where all kinds of kids are more academically successful.

I believe such measures can be implemented without alienating White children or their parents, unless of course they regard any effort to help those who are not well served as a threat to their interests. I'm happy to discuss how we can do this in greater detail, but before I do, I'd like to hear your reaction to what I've described as the problem and potentially the solution.—Pedro

---

Dear Pedro,

The kinds of initiatives that you discuss here strike me as worthy and appealing. Indeed, if we focus solely on your vision of the diversity and equity agenda, most of the reservations I articulated in my last letter would melt away.

You're obviously right about the changing ethnic makeup of America, the significant racial disparities on educational outcomes, and schools having a big part to play in our doing better. I'm with you. I too am a big fan of what Hrabowski has done and of what they're doing at Xavier. So, if that's what we're talking about, there's lots of common ground to be found.

We do disagree on a couple of the particulars. For instance, with regard to your point regarding women in STEM, I agree that we need to be aware of disparities. At the same time, I read the data on that one quite differently. Women now make up nearly 60% of college graduates, after all, and earn the majority of college STEM degrees.[18] So, when it comes to determining what's equitable, some of this comes down to how we understand and interpret data.

Whatever our quibbles on the data, though, we agree on your larger point: America is changing and schools have an obligation to educate, respect, and connect with the kids in their classrooms. As I process the protests brought about by the police killing of George Floyd, for instance, I'm wholly open to the notion that we should explore how to revamp school-based policing. And I'd never thought much about the 160-odd schools still named for Confederate leaders (a serious lapse on my part) but am now convinced we should rename them without delay.[19] You and I have already agreed that there's a need for history and civics instruction that doesn't shrink from the ugly parts of the American story. So there are a number of places where we can get started.

Part of doing so, as you observe, involves equipping teachers to work with students who come to school with experiences and backgrounds that are unlike theirs. Given that teacher education has been harping on this at least since I got my teaching credential three decades ago, without much evident impact, I totally buy the notion that big change is needed. You're also right about the value of cultivating a more racially and ethnically diverse teaching force, though we need to do so in a way that's inclusive and doesn't demean White educators or make them feel unwanted.

Here is where I get to my "but." And it's a big one. It strikes me that there are really two competing definitions of "diversity, equity, and inclusion." The first, which infuses your take, involves seeking ways to serve a more racially diverse student population. I find that approach compelling. But as I suggested in my last letter, it seems that this term is also frequently used as shorthand for a troubling version of "antiracist education" that is itself deeply racist and oppressive.

Although I would very much like to work together in support of many of the suggestions you sketch, I'm adamantly unwilling to sign up for much of what travels under the "antiracism" banner. I'll try to be as concrete as I can. I have in mind, for instance, Robin DiAngelo's insistence in her *New York Times* best-selling book *White Fragility* that "a positive White identity is an impossible goal. White identity is inherently racist; White people do not exist outside the system of White supremacy." As DiAngelo puts it, her solution is to strive to be "a little less White" every day.[20]

Ibram X. Kendi, pop culture star, author of the *New York Times* best seller *How to Be an Antiracist*, and perhaps the leading authority on antiracism, teaches that there is one correct stance on standardized testing (it's racist), pot legalization (it's antiracist), Medicare for All (it's antiracist), and even the capital gains tax rate (low rates are racist).[21] I could go on and on. To Kendi and his followers, there is no room for good-faith argument—there are only disciples and racists. Heck, in Kendi's eyes, I guess we both outed ourselves as "racists" earlier in this correspondence, because he insists that simply using the phrase "achievement gap" is itself racist.

Kendi is funded by a raft of major donors, is all over TV, and has built programs in antiracist research and policy at multiple universities. In his position as founder and director of Boston University's new Center for Antiracist Research, Kendi has promised to "build the world anew" with antiracist research and public scholarship.[22] I can't support visions of diversity or equity that entail helping the likes of DiAngelo and Kendi spread their toxic dogmas to students and educators.

I want to be clear. There are indeed racists who need to be fought, and I'll readily concede that the American Right features more than its share of lunacy, calumny, and conspiracies. No argument there. What I find so troubling, though, is that this stuff isn't being spread by anonymous conspiracy mongers or Twitter trolls but by celebrated keynote speakers and acclaimed authorities.

Kendi's intellectual intolerance or the Smithsonian's embrace of racial stereotypes would seem to represent an assault on core liberal precepts, but too few on the Left agree (or, perhaps, are willing to say that they do). That, I think, is why it's so much tougher than it should be to build broad-based support for the kinds of sensible suggestions you've offered.

Whether in school districts or national policy huddles, the champions of diversity have often given me the impression that they're more intent on promoting ideological agendas than on the more prosaic task of helping teachers educate a changing student population. It can seem like the larger aim is to delegitimize and silence inconvenient ideas or individuals by labeling them as "racist."

We agree that there are real issues to address. That's why I'm all for teacher preparation that takes cultural and social differences seriously, supports that meet kids where they are and affirm who they are, and history that incorporates different voices and is honest about our national failings. As I've said, this suggests a sizable swath of common ground to be explored. But that ground is being rendered uninhabitable by those who have something else in mind.

Am I being unfair? I suspect you see all of this very differently, my friend.

Best,

Rick

Dear Rick,

You opened up quite a number of issues and controversies in your last letter, particularly because you reference individuals whose work you take issue with. Rather than respond to each one of your points, especially as they pertain to the individuals you mentioned, I prefer to stay focused on the issues that I think matter most: How do we create schools where kids, regardless of their backgrounds, are served well? I'm not trying to dodge the controversy, but I prefer to keep our exchange between us rather than discussing the stances and positions taken by others.

I prefer to take this approach because I have generally avoided many of the contentious debates over charter schools, testing, and the issue you raised—what it means to be an antiracist educator—because I don't find them particularly helpful in improving our understanding of the issues. Too often, they degenerate into name-calling, as you've pointed out. To be clear, I don't think that people who favor charter schools or who support standardized testing are necessarily racist. They might be, but not because of their positions on these issues. As I hope we've demonstrated through our exchange, reasonable people can disagree over issues without writing each other off as racists, ideologues, or apologists for the status quo.

Rather than insert myself into these types of controversies, I try to stay focused on learning from the schools, organizations, and practitioners who produce the best outcomes for kids—especially low-income kids of color, who are most often poorly served in schools. We can learn more about the role of race and culture in education from schools that serve kids well than from engaging in abstract debates.

So that returns us to my original question: What can we do to make a real difference for students of color and low-income students? Prior to the pandemic, like you, I traveled a lot. I have had the privilege of visiting and working with schools throughout the world. In New Zealand, I work with a Maori school called Kia Aroha College in Auckland. Founded by Ann Milne, a New Zealand educator, the school is grounded in the culture and languages of Maori and other Polynesian groups. Beyond the excellent academic outcomes the school obtains, it focuses on developing leadership qualities in kids. Their goal is to help kids become "warrior scholars," leaders who possess the understanding to address the challenges facing their communities. For over 20 years they have done just that. When I asked Ann and the other educators what makes the school successful, they attributed it to the clarity of their mission, their willingness to learn from their mistakes, and the fact that they fully embrace the culture of the children. In a society with a history of colonialism and racial oppression, such an approach is not only important educationally but developmentally.

I can name several schools in the United States that do this for Black, Latino, and Native American children, the very children that so many schools struggle in serving. By contrast, the schools that struggle too often blame the children, their parents, and their culture. A culture of blame pervades American education, and I believe it is one of the reasons why we're not making more progress. When we're pointing fingers, it usually means we're not taking responsibility for the factors we control.

By pointing to the schools that serve children of color well, I believe we can get around many of the pointless debates that lead to paralysis and thwart progress. When I take educators to visit schools like these, we shift the focus away from blaming kids, parents, or their culture, and focus instead on creating the conditions that contribute to success.

Is cultural relevance in the curriculum important? The New America Foundation recently issued a report identifying five ways in which student learning is enhanced by culturally responsive teaching (the terms are frequently used interchangeably).[23] The evidence is strong that it makes a difference when educators focus on equity in access to learning opportunities and when they address the social obstacles that might otherwise limit the performance of poor kids, such as housing instability or a lack of support at home. The Learning Policy Institute recently produced a study documenting evidence that shows that such an approach makes a difference.[24]

Where I share your skepticism is on the value of bias training. My skepticism is not based on any doubts that bias and racism are real and pervasive. We have ample evidence that they are. My doubts are based on the fact that I have never seen a school improve or outcomes for kids get better because they did bias training. I have seen White educators get defensive and shut down as a result of participating in antiracist workshops, and I have been to too many schools that claim they've had courageous conversations about race and now want to move on, even though the kids of color they serve are still not achieving.

Let me close with this. I serve on the boards of two excellent community development organizations: Brotherhood/Sister Sol in Harlem, and InnerCity Struggle in East Los Angeles. Both organizations support kids outside of school with mentoring, academic support, and leadership training. Cultural pride, community service, and social responsibility are values they instill in the kids they serve. The remarkable thing about these organizations is that even when their kids attend fairly mediocre schools, the organizations are still able to improve outcomes for the kids they serve because they effectively compensate for what the kids don't receive in school.

I share these examples because, in my opinion, they show the way to a path that can lead us beyond the controversies and conflicts. I'm up for a good fight if it's worth it, but the older I get, the more I know that when we spend energy fighting, we have less energy for solving problems and taking action that can make a difference.—Pedro

---

Dear Pedro,

Although it's clear that we see these issues in very different ways, it also seems that we've found some points of principled agreement.

While I won't pretend to speak for you, I'm left with three takeaways from our exchange.

First, when we're operating at the level of specific problems and practical remedies, we seem able to find swaths of common ground. We know, for instance, that Black and Brown boys are more likely to be disciplined than are other students. Though the evidence suggests that some of this has to do with the rates at which students misbehave, it's also clear that students are indeed treated differently by school systems and personnel.[25] We need to tackle that. As you note, there is a long list of similar issues, such as access to advanced coursework, how we prepare teachers, and so forth. Although we're going to disagree about some of the evidence and specific policies, it's not hard to identify programs that we'd both regard as promising models or to conceive of concrete measures that we'd both endorse.

Second, however much we may agree, as I've said, it's tough for me to imagine collaborating on these issues when it requires partnering with those who attack "Whiteness" as a malevolent force, turn "antiracism" into an ideological dogma, or reject the very values (like hard work and rational thought) that I believe schools should cultivate. I hear you about not wanting to get bogged down in controversial claims when there are important opportunities to do better. That's fair. But I'd argue that there are times when principle requires us to draw a line.

Third, I quite like the notion of "warrior scholar" that you surface in your last letter. Though I'm not 100% sure I'm doing justice to the phrase, it evokes for me an image of schools invested in a vision of excellence that's rooted in the values of the communities they serve. That seems like an extraordinarily healthy way to promote diversity and inclusion. I love the idea of schools that teach students to take pride in their heritage and culture and to proudly view themselves as valued members of their community. This is what parochial schools so successfully set out to do once upon a time. If schools serving students of a particular race, faith, or culture can better cultivate excellent scholars and citizens by celebrating their history and honoring their traditions, that strikes me as a very good thing. And it also seems to me a very different—and much better—project than teaching White students that their identity is noxious or seeking to dictate an Orwellian catalog of impermissible thought.

   Once again, I've enjoyed the conversation and learned from it. We obviously haven't resolved the big tension that accompanies the energetic push for "antiracist" training, but we've surfaced bits of common ground and stumbled into some useful exchanges along the way. Though that may not be a lot, it's not nothing.

   Best,
   Rick

CHAPTER 11

Teacher Pay

There's broad sentiment that teachers should be paid more but a great deal of uncertainty about how that should be done or how to make it happen. Teacher pay is another place where Rick and Pedro find a surprising amount of agreement. Rick suggests that good teachers are sorely underpaid; argues that the solution has less to do with spending more than with approaching pay differently; and calls for combining increases in teacher pay with larger changes to staffing, teacher roles, and benefits. Pedro, too, strongly endorses efforts to boost teacher pay while suggesting that it needs to be part of an effort to "promote teacher professionalism" and address "working conditions in schools." Pedro argues that teachers need better training, enhanced professional development, and additional support staff. Rick is open to all of this but notes that the growth in nonteaching staff has significantly outpaced the growth in enrollment over the past several decades, and fears that—absent changes in work roles and school routines—more hires will add administrative bloat rather than make a real difference for students or teachers. Critical questions include whether teacher pay should be raised, how any increases should be designed, and what this would mean for school staffing.

Dear Pedro,

When it comes to schooling, pretty much every conversation eventually comes back to the teachers doing the work. Given that, it's probably a good time to talk teacher pay.

As you well know, school reformers didn't spend a lot of time on teacher pay in the 2000s and 2010s. They were so intently focused on evaluation and revamping tenure that issues of pay tended to feel like an afterthought. There just weren't many cases during the No Child Left Behind and Race to the Top eras, where big efforts to rethink teacher pay were part of the larger reform push. I can think of a few instances here and there—in Denver, Washington, D.C., and Newark—but those were more the exception than the rule. And I'm hard-pressed to think of a single state where policymakers really took up teacher pay in a big way.

This was a strange state of affairs. After all, teachers have legitimate gripes when it comes to pay. Real, inflation-adjusted teacher pay actually declined by 2% between 1992 and 2014.[1] In nearly one-fourth of states, the average teacher earns less than $50,000 a year.[2] Good teachers are woefully underpaid, have few attractive professional pathways, and don't get the respect or opportunities they deserve.

Thus, we probably shouldn't have been surprised by the wave of teacher strikes that began when West Virginia's teachers launched a 9-day walkout in early 2018.[3] The state's teachers, with median pay of less than $45,000 a year, sought a modest 5% pay bump. After they got it, similarly successful strikes followed in Oklahoma, Arizona, and elsewhere. Over the next few years, teacher strikes became common occurrences in major cities, including Los Angeles, Denver, and Chicago.

Here's where I'm at: Teachers should be paid more, and terrific teachers should be paid much more. I also think, however, that it's inaccurate to suggest that pay is low because taxpayers are unwilling to provide funding. For instance, real, after-inflation school spending increased by 27% between 1992 and 2014 (a period encompassing the 2001 dot-com crash and the 2008 Great Recession).[4] Where did the money go? Districts spent the biggest share of the new funds on additional staff, health care, and retirement benefits. In other words, they spent the money on employees—but not on boosting teacher pay.

For example, in West Virginia, even as student enrollment declined between 1992 and 2014, nonteaching staff actually grew by 10%. That was broadly true across the land. Nationally, while student enrollment grew 20% over that period, nonteaching staff grew more than twice as much.[5] I'd argue that a lot of these administrative and support staff are not a great investment, but that superintendents and school boards are loath to eliminate these positions once people are in them. The result was a lot of new spending that could have gone into raising pay instead went into adding bodies.

At various times, we've tried reform without dollars and dollars without reform. Both approaches consistently disappoint. That's why I'm for boosting teacher pay, but only as part of a bigger bargain. I think a serious deal has at least four parts.

First, we need to be clear that <u>teaching is crucial work, and schools</u> <u>that want to attract and keep</u> talented professionals need to pay them <u>accordingly.</u> This may require additional funds.

Second, new spending should help promote teacher professionalism by creating opportunities for skilled, hardworking teachers. Too many terrific teachers spend summers tending bar or painting houses. Any deal should involve asking how we might start to shift teaching from a 10-month gig to a year long role in which accomplished educators develop curricula, coach colleagues, and much more.

Third, a boost in teacher pay needs to be paired with a push to trim bureaucratic bloat. As long as schools keep adding nonteaching staff twice as fast as they add students, finding the funds to significantly raise teacher pay is a Sisyphean task. After all, 80% of school spending is for salaries and benefits.[6] Trimming a dozen low-level administrators can fund a $10,000 per year bump for 100 or more classroom educators.

Finally, we need to overhaul benefits. For every 10 bucks contributed to teacher pensions, 7 pay down past pension debt and just 3 underwrite benefits for current teachers.[7] As you know better than I do, the Los Angeles school system is spending more than $2,300 per student each year on health benefits for teachers, a figure that keeps rising.[8] Such obligations make it hugely difficult to give teachers a sizable bump in take-home pay.

I want to see teachers earn a lot more, but I also want to be confident that new dollars are being spent in ways that will serve students. If we're willing to make some tough compromises, it's possible to boost all teacher pay by 20% to 30% or more, pay terrific teachers six figures, leave class sizes stable, and do it all with measured tax increases.

I'll be most curious to see where you think I'm on track and where you think I've gone off the rails.

Best,

Rick

Hi, Rick,

We're together on the need to raise teacher pay. It's hard to recruit smart, dedicated college students into the teaching profession when we know that many new teachers are barely surviving on a teacher's salary. In cities like New York, San Francisco, Boston, and Los Angeles, where housing costs are high, it's really a problem. For example, in Los Angeles, the average monthly rent for a one-bedroom apartment is $2,000, but the starting salary for a teacher is just over $50,000.[9] This means that teachers are spending 50% of their income on housing. I also hear from teachers in rural areas who are struggling to get by. Many work at more than one job just to pay their bills. Some urban districts are looking into ways to subsidize teacher housing to offset the meager pay, but it will take a while for these ideas to bear fruit.

The issues you've raised further complicate the concerns related to teacher pay: rising pension costs, seniority systems that place new teachers at a significant disadvantage, and districts prioritizing administrative costs over salaries for teachers. I don't know how easily any of these issues can be resolved by legislation, but we've got to try. The strikes in West Virginia, Arizona, and Kentucky showed us that there is considerable public support for teachers in red and blue states. But it shouldn't take a strike for teachers to be treated fairly.

I think you're onto something when you think in terms of packaging reforms that link increases in teacher pay to other changes in how we finance public education. It's important to keep in mind that the pension problem you mentioned isn't an issue only for teachers. Many states are struggling to cover pensions for all kinds of public employees, including police and firefighters. However, if we put those issues aside to just focus on the teachers, I can think of several related issues that could be combined to make the profession more attractive and sustainable:

1. We should lift the base pay of new teachers so that their starting salaries are equivalent to those of other professions that require a 4-year degree. I think we should pay teachers at rates that are similar to nurses and police officers. Right now, they're paid about $10,000 less than professionals in these fields.[10] This would help with recruitment and demonstrate concrete support and respect for the profession.

2. We should reduce some of the authority of local school districts to build in cost-of-living raises and merit increases through state legislation. This would reduce the inequities in teacher pay among school districts and increase the likelihood that people will stay in the profession longer. This would eliminate some of the haggling and strained relations

created by collective bargaining and provide some assurance
to new teachers that they can earn a decent living over time if
they stick with the job. We can't afford to lose good teachers
just because they want to have a family, buy a house, or
purchase a car when it's obvious that these things won't be
possible on a teacher's salary.

3. We need to promote teacher professionalism. That means
   extending the time to tenure to at least three years so that we
   are certain that those who end up with job security (which I
   feel they deserve) are good and committed to the profession.
   Ideally, we should make the hiring requirements tougher so we
   send a clear message that we want highly skilled individuals in
   the profession. Of course, this won't be possible in areas where
   there are teacher shortages. But in big cities, we should pay
   people with degrees in math and science or specializations in
   English as a second language and special education more.

4. Most of all, teacher compensation is about more than just
   pay, which is why we need to focus on working conditions in
   schools. Keeping class size down, making sure that schools are
   safe and orderly, and ensuring that each teacher has time in
   their schedule to prepare and meet with colleagues will make
   the profession more attractive. Most people who leave teaching
   prematurely talk about the conditions at their school that made
   the job unbearable, even more than their pay. I don't think
   legislation can mandate better conditions in schools, but this
   should be a priority for superintendents if they want to retain
   good teachers.

There's a lot more territory to cover on this topic. I look forward to
hearing from you.—Pedro

Dear Pedro,

We both want to boost teacher pay, promote teacher professionalism, and address pensions along with pay. So what would it take to
move forward here?

For me, the biggest obstacle is the fact that schools don't show
much evidence of making good use of teachers' time—which makes it

hard to be confident that higher pay will translate into student learning. This isn't the teachers' fault (even if collective bargaining agreements bear some of the blame), but it's become their problem.

Gifted veterans and wide-eyed novices have similar duties, with each taking a turn watching the cafeteria or assisting with bus duty. Teachers spend inordinate amounts of time filling out forms, filing paperwork, and sitting through mindless meetings and trainings. Classroom instruction is usually a pastiche of powerful learning, well-designed lessons, rote lecture, busywork, distractions, and wasted time.

When I work with teacher leaders and ask them to list what they do in a typical day, it's no trick at all for a group to quickly generate a list of 60 or more tasks. Researchers have found that teachers are asked to cope with 2,000 classroom interruptions a year, costing nearly 2 weeks of class time.[11] And although no one believes that all the things teachers do are equally valuable, the teachers I work with almost invariably say that they've never been part of a serious effort to unpack their workday in order to better focus on the things that matter most. A reckoning on time and productivity has to be part of the push on pay.

This is a big part of the teacher pay equation because schools spend most of their money paying personnel—as I noted in my last letter, 80% of spending goes to salaries and benefits, and more than two-thirds of that goes to teachers.[12] It's hard to justify paying a teacher $100,000 a year if they're spending lots of time doing rote secretarial tasks. It gets a lot easier when that teacher is devising dynamic lessons, mentoring kids, connecting with families, or helping elevate their colleagues.

I think there's a useful analogy to medicine here. A little over a century ago, there was no such thing as a medical specialty. Today, there are more than 100 specialties.[13] This kind of exquisite, expensive expertise is possible in large part because medicine has designed practices that ensure that these physicians maximize the time spent actually applying their finely honed skills. Meanwhile, routine tasks are taken up by less costly physician's assistants, nurse practitioners, emergency medical technicians, and the like.

This kind of role redesign could make good sense in schools. After all, successful teaching involves a remarkable array of know-how, skill, and empathy. Teachers are asked to do everything from applying sophisticated expertise in early literacy to forging trust with a troubled teen. Teachers may have no idea how to do some of what's being asked. Meanwhile, those with particular strengths are asked to shoulder additional burdens, typically without recognition or compensation. And teachers are tasked with doing a mix of all of these things, while also making copies, wrestling with classroom technology, filing paperwork, monitoring hallways, and doing dozens of other things.

Rethinking how tasks are organized, how the talents of individual staff are maximized, and how responsibilities are assigned and compensated could allow schools to ramp up pay while making far better use of the talent they employ.[14] For me, rethinking pay is part of the larger opportunity to staff schools in ways that better support and instruct kids.

Best,

Rick

Hi, Rick,

I like the idea of paying more for teachers who take on greater responsibility. Some districts have done this for department chairs and for those who serve as mentors to new teachers. I think it's a shame that we lose so many great teachers to administration or to other lines of work simply because they need to earn more money. Finding ways to keep excellent teachers in classrooms and getting them to serve as a source of support to other teachers should be a priority.

I would go further. I think we should offer incentive pay to teachers who are willing to work in hard-to-staff urban and rural schools. Ideally, the incentives should go to people with a track record of effectiveness. Yet too many organizations incentivize—via financial rewards, prestige, or the like—underprepared teachers to enter the most high-needs schools. This is one of my criticisms of Teach For America. Nearly all of the corps members I've known have been dedicated, smart, and committed. But almost all have been unprepared and overwhelmed by the work they were assigned. That should be expected. It takes more than enthusiasm to be a good teacher, particularly for "high-need" students. If we could find ways to get teachers who have demonstrated expertise and effectiveness to work with "high-need" kids or schools, it could make a big difference.

I agree with you that the key is to avoid burning teachers out. Aside from the issues surrounding compensation and attrition that we

discussed before, many people do not realize how emotionally, psycho-
logically, and physically taxing teaching can be. In many of the schools
I work with, I see the toll it takes on teachers, especially when they
work in underresourced schools. So many tell me that they are sleep
deprived, that they often feel guilty about ignoring the needs of their
own families because they prioritize their students' needs, and that
they are feeling worn out.

We have got to find ways to make teaching sustainable, and this
goes far beyond how much teachers are paid. The recent teacher strikes
in Los Angeles, Chicago, Denver, and Oakland focused less on compensation and more on the need for social workers and nurses in schools.
It's clear that teachers can see how the conditions in their schools affect their students and their ability to do their jobs. We have to make
sure that the public understands what they are going through.

The coronavirus has reminded us that our public schools—including
both teachers and support staff—are critical parts of the social safety
net for kids. In some cases, they are the only place where children are
guaranteed a meal. At the beginning of quarantine, I spent a couple of
mornings giving out meals to kids and families in Los Angeles at a
school in Koreatown because I heard they needed volunteers. I was
there with teachers and staff who were volunteering during their spring
break to get meals to kids.

Let me put this another way: You seem to think that adding nonteaching staff has been a problem—I actually think it's part of the
solution. Teachers need help in addressing the needs of kids. In my
opinion, paying teachers a decent salary is just the starting point for
adequately supporting them and our public schools. Stay healthy, my
friend.—Pedro

Dear Pedro,

As I read your take on overwhelmed, frustrated, and ill-equipped
teachers, I kept thinking, "True, true, true." When I was writing my
Cage-Busting Teacher book a few years back, I was struck time and
again by just that frustration—on the part of accomplished and appren-
tice teachers alike. Given that these challenges tend to be especially
acute in hard-to-staff schools, I'm certainly open to strategies that use
incentives or pay adjustments.

Although quality training can certainly make a difference, I worry that teacher preparation is frequently unhelpful and often more about the ideological agendas of teacher educators than practical classroom tools. And I think we can agree that decades of research show that professional development has little practical impact on what teachers do or on what students learn.

You suggest that a lack of support staff is a major challenge. Now, I have a lot of sympathy for your argument, but *only* if new hires are part of a coherent effort to reallocate responsibilities and provide purposeful, cost-effective support for teachers and students. They can't just represent additions to a shambolic status quo.

To make this work, positions need to be designed (or redesigned) to reduce the burdens on instructional staff and offer students essential supports. Unfortunately, experience has left me dubious that these hires will be used that way. Too often, I see counselors used not as resources to mentor and coach kids, but as test proctors, substitute teachers, and warm bodies.

More generally, I'm not sure that many noninstructional job descriptions are necessarily well designed for the roles they're intended to play. And I'm just not confident that the people in these roles always bring the skill sets that are needed to make a difference. For instance, experience has left me unconvinced that a lot of instructional coaches are necessarily good at coaching or have a clear sense of how to improve instruction. The job title sounds good, but it doesn't reflect the work that's actually being done. Perhaps students would be better served by fewer "counselors" on staff and more community members who—even absent conventional certifications—may be better positioned to know, mentor, and support students.

Ultimately, I'm skeptical that more new staff will matter unless we rethink the work. If we do, we may decide that we'd rather spend less on these positions and more on crafting new, year-round, high-impact, more purposeful roles for instructional staff.

For clarity, I'll offer one tiny illustration of the sort of thing I'm suggesting. Some teachers have a gift for home visits and speaking to parents. Many others do not. Right now, teacher–parent contact is sporadic and uneven; it's just one more thing that every teacher is asked to squeeze in and that someone in the central administration is tasked with coordinating. Here's an alternative approach. Say that one member of each instructional team in a middle school was offered the chance to become a 12-month employee, with a 30% or 35% bump in pay, while assuming responsibility for visiting the team's incoming families during the summer, developing parental outreach routines, supporting colleagues, and coordinating parental contact during the school year. Such an approach could lighten the load on other staff, help forge stronger teacher–parent bonds, and allow effective educators to be rewarded for work they find important and fulfilling.

Anyway, you've raised the vital issue of teacher education. I'm curious: How do you view the quality of teacher preparation today, and what would it take for it to deliver on our aspirations?

Best,

Rick

Dear Rick,

We started this exchange focusing on teacher pay and whether or not it's fair. That opens up the topic of what we do to support teachers in their work. So let me respond in some detail to two of the issues you raised in the last letter: problems with professional development and ineffective teacher education at the university level. I want to share what I think is the best approach to addressing both issues.

On the subject of teacher education, I think there's no denying that there's a need for improvement. The gap between what teachers learn while they are in credential programs and what they actually do when they are hired by schools is too wide. Additionally, even the best teacher education programs don't produce highly effective teachers. We produce novices, some of whom are quite good and promising, but all of whom will need lots of support to get better. To become a master teacher, a teacher must be (1) highly skilled in teaching content or imparting critical skills such as reading, (2) creative so that they can effectively engage their students, and (3) great at building strong relationships with kids.

The best teacher-education programs provide their students with grounding in how to do all three of these things. They do this through residency programs that eliminate the gap between what teachers learn at the university and what they do in the classroom. Closing that gap is essential because new teachers have abstract ideas about teaching (some of which may be useful while others are not), but too often they struggle to implement these ideas with real kids in classrooms they control (or are supposed to control). When university faculty who have expertise in teaching are present as coaches or mentors in the classroom with student-teachers, they are able to respond in real time to mistakes and challenges that arise.

In this way, teacher education begins to resemble the best aspects of medical education. New resident interns don't perform heart surgery. In fact, when they're starting out, they don't even take a patient's temperature unless a seasoned physician is present. Similarly, we should not expect new teachers to be effective with the most challenging students (as I've stated previously, this is the biggest problem with the Teach For America model). Instead, like medical interns, we should gradually increase the nature of the challenges new teachers face while providing lots of guidance from seasoned professionals.

Similarly, though I agree that much of what teachers receive in the form of professional development is useless and ineffective, it doesn't mean that teachers don't need guidance or support. A big part of the problem is that all teachers receive the same training. This is ridiculous because teachers have different needs. Some need support in understanding and teaching academic content, some need pedagogical support to make their lessons more impactful and engaging, and some need help in developing positive relationships with their students.

Ideally, professional development (PD) for teachers should be differentiated and tailored to meet the needs of individual teachers. Unfortunately, I've only seen one school where teachers had differentiated PD. More often than not, all teachers get the same thing, whether or not they need it. PD should include coaching in the classroom, and it should provide numerous opportunities for new teachers to reflect on what they are doing. When all of these components are present, teachers generally appreciate the value of professional development.

The best PD I've ever seen gives teachers the opportunity to analyze student work together and to discuss the implications of what kids produce for their teaching. I have seen teachers become more aware of how their instruction affects student learning when they get to examine student work on a regular basis with their colleagues.

This is ultimately what great professional development for teachers should do.

Clearly, there's a need to systematically improve teacher education and professional development. Several states seem to be trying to address this need. I've been particularly impressed by initiatives to improve teacher education and professional development in Virginia, Maryland, and California. I hope we can make this happen on a larger scale, for the sake of teachers and students everywhere.—Pedro

CHAPTER 12

COVID-19

A few months into Rick and Pedro's correspondence, the nation was gripped by a global pandemic that shuttered schools across the land and disrupted learning for more than 50 million students. The result was a massive experiment in remote learning and a stark reminder of the broader purposes that schools serve—resurfacing issues that Rick and Pedro explored at the very beginning of their conversation. They discuss what to make of this unprecedented moment. Pedro is particularly struck by "the equity issues raised by the pandemic" and muses, "if there's a silver lining to come from this experience with respect to education, I hope it's a return to a focus on education that stimulates and inspires kids." Rick largely agrees, while pointing out that the national lockdown created a massive opportunity for the reflection that's often absent amid the daily routine of educators and would-be school reformers. Rick adds that the difficulty schools had pivoting to remote learning cast a harsh spotlight on how bureaucratic rules and familiar routines can fail to serve students well. Key themes include the promise of remote learning, what lessons should be taken from the coronavirus shutdown, and how to judge when rules and routines are no longer serving students well.

Dear Pedro,

We're having this exchange in the midst of a pandemic that has thrown our world off its axis. I guess we should talk about it, especially given that we're both going through this as parents with school-age kids.

The thing that's most struck me about the school shutdowns is how little the initial response had to do with the way we've long talked about schools. For much of the past two decades, policymakers and philanthropists pushed schools to emphasize "college readiness," boost reading and math scores, and evaluate teachers.

Schools that did these things were lauded, and those that didn't were lambasted. Few leading this charge spent a lot of time asking whether this was a sensible, useful, or accurate way to judge how well schools were doing.

And yet, after close to two decades of this, it was remarkable to see the COVID-19 school closures put front and center all the stuff schools do that isn't captured by test scores. Suddenly, we were reminded that schools feed millions of kids, ease pressures on parents, provide a crucial source of routine and relationships, and sponsor activities that give kids a productive outlet for youthful energy. When all this was swept away, millions of families were suddenly at sea.

There's much to be said about remote learning and how effectively schools did or didn't respond to the challenge. There are important questions about how rules and regulations may have hindered an effective response and how socioeconomic inequities may have aggravated the challenges.

But I'm inclined to start by just musing on how abruptly the habits of two decades of school reform screeched to a standstill when schools were suddenly taken away. When teachers marched in parks with signs telling their students how much they missed them, parents drove across town so that kids could wave and cheer. This wasn't about instructional prowess. It was about the human core of schooling.

Best,
Rick

Rick,

Greetings from quarantine!

Like you, I'm juggling working from home, serving as a surrogate teacher to my 8-year-old, foraging for food in supermarkets that have been stripped bare (with no toilet paper!), trying to get some exercise, and on top of it all, trying to enjoy a chance to be with my family. Even as I gripe about confinement, I reflect on how fortunate I am compared to so many others. My family is not sick, I'm still working and receiving a paycheck, and I have the ability to help educate my daughter because my wife and I are college-educated people with the time and know-how to do it. Many others don't have these privileges.

I agree that the pandemic has provided us with a critical reminder of why schools are important. Instead of being concerned about achievement on standardized tests, we're concerned with ensuring that all kids have access to learning. Given that many kids lack access to laptops and Internet at home, the pandemic has exposed why the digital divide is such a big problem.

The stay-at-home orders have also reminded us, as you noted, that kids need schools for socialization and parents need school so that they can work. Although a relatively small number of home schoolers had opted to keep their kids out of school long before the pandemic, many other parents have taken for granted that school is where kids learn vital social skills like how to cooperate, make friends, deal with people from different backgrounds, and handle conflict. Now, they have to figure this stuff out on their own, and many are struggling. It's especially stressful if you're expected to be productive at home.

In addition, I too have concerns about education during this period. I worry that too many kids are spending too much time on screens, and not because they're doing interesting educational activities but because they're playing video games and watching YouTube and TikTok. I worry that there are lots of kids whose parents can't help them with learning, who don't have access to the Internet, and who are living in crowded apartments where there's no space for learning.

If there's a silver lining to come from this experience with respect to education, I hope it's a return to a focus on education that stimulates and inspires kids. I've seen some great examples of science projects that have kids outside studying bugs, and research projects on the origins of the pandemic. Perhaps this experience will remind us that when we get kids actively involved in learning, they are more likely to become motivated to learn on their own.

What do you think?—Pedro

Dear Pedro,

It turns out that the middle of a pandemic is an exceptionally good time for reflection. Who would've thought it? The coronavirus has slowed life down to a crawl. I've suddenly found myself taking long walks and with a calendar cleared of travel and meetings. The result is a lot of time for contemplation.

It's got me thinking that, when it comes to school improvement, reflection is in mighty short supply. Rather, there's a premium on doing things fast. Teachers race to cover required content. Schools sprint to improve performance before spring assessments. Districts leap from one improvement model to the next. And policymakers and advocates rush to enact bold reforms.

There's not much space to think practically about the purpose of education or what that means for how educators should do their work. There's not much time to consider what measures of reading and math performance really tell us. And there's little patience for figuring out why the *last* improvement strategy didn't deliver before blazing ahead with the next.

I suspect we've paid a steep price. Urgency can be a powerful force for change but we've been in such a rush that bad ideas got a free pass and healthy scrutiny got dismissed as truculence. I can't help but wonder if a more measured pace might've ultimately gotten us farther, faster—and with a lot less swerving and swearing.

This moment provides an opportunity to reset some of our rhythms. But I don't know that we'll seize it. My inbox is stuffed with missives from vendors hawking their remote learning wares, advocates touting their agendas, and funders racing to promote new priorities. I don't see a lot of evidence of measured deliberation. District leaders tell me that they've little time for rumination or re-appraisal because they're scrambling to deliver meals and online instruction. And, on top of it all, we've seemingly developed a knack for turning everything, even a global pandemic, into one more front of our raging culture wars.

Indeed, one obstacle to serious reflection is that it's tough to engage in measured appraisal of how schools are doing. As I've tried to provide such assessments, I've found that even tempered criticism can be interpreted by superintendents, school boards, and teachers as vicious slander.

But we need to be able to talk about both the good and the bad if we're to make sense of what's happening or to learn from it. On the one hand, we should appreciate our teachers and respect schools and systems that have stepped up. Many accounts rightly depict educators as "heroes." On the other hand, there's plenty of cause for frustration with responses that have frequently seemed less than heroic.

Heck, my local Arlington Public Schools opted to combat concerns about equity by ordering teachers not to teach new content this spring.[1] Your local Los Angeles school system negotiated a shutdown agreement with teachers that maintained full pay while cutting their workday to 4 hours and specifying that they needn't do any live, online instruction.[2] Even as we approach the end of the school year, fully one-third of school districts still don't expect teachers to do any teaching at all.[3]

Learning from what we're going through will require taking the time to make sense of the good, the bad, and the ugly. That's easier said than done. Do you think we're up to the challenge?

Best,

Rick

Dear Rick,

I can't agree more about the need to reflect on what we're doing. I'm privileged because my job is secure and I can continue paying my bills, unlike millions of others. Like you, I appreciate the additional time with my family, and it's made me realize that I want to do less after this quarantine ends: less travel, fewer projects, fewer meetings, and so forth. I want to do things that feel rewarding and impactful—both personally and professionally—and too often the stuff that consumes my time is neither.

My hope is that educators have time for this type of reflection, too, even as they're also expected to "deliver" instruction to kids at home. Virtual learning is totally different from classroom instruction because you can't make kids comply by threatening to fail them or send them to the office. We've relied on fear of failure as a motivator for too long, and in this learning space it simply won't work (it didn't work for lots of kids before, either). If kids get bored and restless, if they are more interested in staring and making faces at their peers (like my daughter) than they are in listening to the teacher, or if they simply feel unmotivated to get their work done, there's not much teachers can do.

If teachers get the time to reflect on what they're teaching and have the opportunity to be creative, then virtual teaching and learning could spark real change. Some teachers have always been creative, but too many others were pressured into focusing on test preparation and simply covering material and rarely had the time to consider tapping into the curiosity of kids.

There's good research showing that curiosity can help kids to become self-motivated learners and reduce the gap between affluent and low-income kids.[4] I believe that rather than focusing narrowly on achievement, we should be focused on getting kids stimulated and motivated so that they want to read and continue learning long after class is over. This may seem idealistic, but it actually works that way now for lots of kids. I know it could be that way for more kids because all kids are naturally curious when they're small. Of course, as they get older, we enter into a fierce competition with video games, YouTube, and social media. Maria Montessori, the Italian physician who came up with a novel approach to educating small children, understood this. She knew that kids will learn on their own when provided with the right stimulation.

One last thought: The equity issues raised by the pandemic are still on my mind. Aside from the access issues I raised before (e.g., no access to Internet at home, no laptops, no one to help you with your work, no place to get your work done, etc.), I'm sure you've also seen the data showing that African Americans and Latinos are dying in much greater numbers in many parts of the country.[5] Many of them are "essential workers." Isn't it ironic that so many of the essential workers—farmworkers, grocery store clerks, meatpackers, and health care workers—are paid so little? Isn't it ironic that so many of the people who receive the highest salaries—athletes, entertainers, financiers, and so forth—aren't essential at all? I believe that our inequality and our racial disparities not only compromise our health, but they also threaten our future as a nation. Racial disparities in health conditions such as asthma, heart disease, and mortality rates mirror racial disparities in educational outcomes. Will this pandemic increase our willingness to address both, or will we simply accept them as an unfortunate part of life in America?—Pedro

---

Dear Pedro,

Your point about disparities in income and health are well taken. You and I are immensely fortunate that our jobs allow us to correspond from the comforts of home even as essential workers are out keeping our streets clean, our power on, and food on our tables. And, as you note, much of this comes back to education.

Great schools can help us start to erase these troubling disparities. And yet school is a spirit-sapping purgatory for so many youths, perhaps especially those who need schools to throw open the doors of opportunity.

I've found myself noodling as to why it's so tough to keep students excited about learning. After all, curiosity is such a primal impulse. One of the wonderful (and maddening) things about little kids is the constant barrage of questions. "What's this, Daddy?" "What's that, Daddy?" "Why can't I stick it in my mouth, Daddy?" The questions are incessant, hilarious, and exhausting.

It's befuddling that we've designed schools that seem intent on stomping flat that hardwired fascination with the world around us. Kids start off so interested in, well, everything, and it's bizarre to see that peter out during their school years. This spring has reminded me of all this once again.

With kids quarantined and stuck without sports or friends, one might've imagined remote schooling would've provided an engaging diversion. Yet hardly any of the parents, teachers, or students I've heard from have described it that way. Instead, most described remote schooling as a lot of tedious busywork. When I asked about bright spots, I heard that it was easy and flexible, not that it was absorbing or fun.

And I don't quite know who to blame. Teachers? Parents? iPhones? Pop culture? I mean, figuring out how to engagingly educate even a single kid is tricky work, and then we've charged schools with all manner of additional responsibilities—from food preparation to managing major bus fleets. As our present moment reminds us, just juggling the logistics of all this is no simple task.

I believe that teachers and schools need to do better. Yet the truth is that I've spent years in high school and college classrooms and still find that keeping just *two* little kids on task or even under control is frequently more than I can manage. There's the constant swirl of chatter, laughter, tears, and questions, and it starts all over every 20 or 30 minutes. Simply getting them to read or work independently can be one long game of 5-minute intervals, intermingled with whining, giggling, and bad decisions.

I look back over the decades to teaching in Baton Rouge, when I'd have 30 high schoolers in a classroom, and I wonder how I made it through the day. For all my frustrations with the state of schooling, I'm fully conscious of how amazingly tough it can be to engage a classroom of kids. And that was even before the constant distractions posed by text messages, Twitter spats, and TikTok trends.

So, I'm trying to reconcile two impulses: the conviction that schools should be far more enlivening than so many are, and the reminder that the daily work of teaching can be a wearying grind even for the most committed teachers. And I fear that I've no special wisdom when it comes to resolving that tension.

Perhaps the dislocations of this spring and our dismal experiment in remote learning will spark some sorely needed thinking on all this. That may be too much to ask . . . but I'm looking for silver linings here.

Best,

Rick

Rick,

Like you, I'm struggling with the challenge of educating a child at home, which you might think shouldn't be too hard since I'm also a former teacher, but it's proving to be much more difficult than either my wife or I expected. My daughter is very social. She loves speaking in class, interacting with peers, and when given the chance, helping other kids to learn. Sitting in front of a laptop doing lessons via Zoom just isn't working for her. I imagine there must be many kids like her. I also know that there are many kids who prefer virtual learning. Introverts who may find the social aspects of school to be difficult may prefer virtual learning. This is another reason why it's so complicated to meet the diverse needs of children in school.

I've also been thinking about what should be different after the pandemic and when schools open again. We've both been critical about the schemes designed to fix schools that are rarely evaluated, about instruction that is too often more focused on coverage of content than deep engagement with core ideas, and by the way we've allowed standardized testing to drive everything. Given that tests have been suspended for this spring, what else should we reconsider or do differently?

I have a few thoughts. In several webinars, I have encouraged educators to treat this moment as an opportunity for a reset. Instead of simply telling kids what to do, we've got to work harder at getting them more motivated and engaged. Teachers will have to check in on the mental health of their students because, as we know, isolation is taking a toll on many of them. Many kids have been stressed out by the pandemic and the economic challenges their families face. Additionally, it's likely that many kids may not have learned very much while they've been learning at home. Should schools try to play catch-up by packing in more instruction, or should they simply accept what's happened and pick up from where kids are? Finally, because parents can't return to work until schools reopen, there's now greater awareness of how vital schools are to our economy. How should this realization affect the way we support schools?

Quarantine has given me time to come up with lots of questions and even a few thoughts about how this interruption to the status quo could change things for the better. Perhaps you've seen images of animals returning to parks and other areas because human activity has all but ceased. Perhaps educators can use this as an opportunity to restore a focus on the "whole" child so that learning, play, and the arts are central. This is what my friend Sir Ken Robinson, who recently passed away, has argued was missing from too many schools. I worry that if we don't use this pandemic as an opportunity to change things for the better in our society, then the hardships we've grown accustomed to are likely to worsen.–Pedro

---

Dear Pedro,

You're right that the biggest question to emerge from this experience may well be, What should we do differently?

I'm of two minds on this. On the one hand, I'm not crazy about the impulse to treat tragedy as a political "opportunity." On the other hand, at times like this, it's incredibly human in the best of ways to ask how we can take something good from it. Otherwise, as you say, it's too easy to think that all the anguish and sacrifice was for nothing.

With that, here are a couple thoughts on what we should reconsider or do differently.

First, the last few months have starkly illustrated that good schools offer the kind of community, connection, and support that doesn't readily translate to virtual interaction. That loss is especially important for students in unstable, unsafe, or abusive homes and for those who lack strong adult role models in their lives. Enthusiasm for the possibilities of online learning is fine, but we need to fully appreciate the human dynamics that make schools into special places.

Second, I find the perils of runaway educational bureaucracy especially evident at times like this. We've seen school districts failing to offer any instruction for weeks on end due to fears (justified or not) that they'd violate rules governing special education or equitable provision.[6] Philadelphia's leadership, for instance, kicked off the shutdown by telling principals that teachers should *not* teach, take attendance, or evaluate student work because the district couldn't be certain that services would be equally "available to all children."[7] And, remarkably, most states allowed districts to ignore special education in their remote learning plans due to the "concern," researchers blandly observed, that doing more "could expose them to lawsuits."[8]

Most of the time, education policymaking suffers from a basic asymmetry. It's easy to make the case for expansive new protections, even as fears about red tape can come across as callous or abstract. But this spring has helped illustrate how blunderbuss rules can fuel paralysis among educational leaders. When policies designed to protect students compel educational leaders to instruct teachers not to educate kids, those rules deserve a closer look.

Third, this spring's experience raises the issue of just what it means to be a "teacher" and the implications for policy and practice. Normally, public education is quite prescriptive about certification standards—with plenty of school systems evincing little enthusiasm for nontraditional teachers, local tutors, or community volunteers. Yet, suddenly, and without hesitation, schools have deputized tens of millions of untrained parents to serve as their kids' primary instructors. That suggests that we can perhaps find ways to create more useful, complementary roles for noneducators and volunteers.

Anyway, that's my first reaction when asked what we should be doing differently. How do you see this?

Best,

Rick

Rick,

Thanks for sharing your thoughts on what might be different in education after the virus. I've also been thinking about what will be different after quarantine. I've received a number of questions from reporters who are writing stories about the gaps in learning opportunities between poor and affluent kids.[9] They're wondering how we'll make up for learning loss in communities where lots of kids don't even have access to the Internet at home.

In response, I've tried to encourage reporters and educators not to think of learning in purely linear terms. I know that's how we typically measure learning: the number of minutes of instructional time, the number of units covered in a class, the number of days kids are in school, and so forth. Our assumption, or maybe our hope, is that a year in school translates to a year of academic growth. Of course, this is not how it works for lots of kids. I don't mean to suggest that our traditional measures are irrelevant, just that they don't actually measure how much a child has learned. We've all seen kids who make dramatic progress in a subject in a short period of time, and we've seen kids who seem to get stuck in their learning regardless of how much instructional time they receive. For this reason, I think we should be more concerned with the quality of students' learning experiences rather than the amount of time they are in class.

I worry that if we fixate on measuring the loss, we will accentuate the anxieties of parents who want to make sure that their kids keep up with (or get ahead of) other kids. I think it makes more sense to encourage parents to get their kids reading independently, working on research projects, writing in a journal, and undertaking creative projects that engage and inspire them. For example, my daughter recently started her own podcast called "Things Just Got Interesting." I'm not sure how she came up with the title, but I like it. So far, it consists of interviews with her mom, grandma, and a cousin in Italy and her musings about the pandemic and life in quarantine. What I like about it is that she is using technology creatively rather than simply watching YouTube and TikTok. She's shared her podcast with kids in her class and several have been inspired to produce shows of their own.

If more kids become empowered as learners and more parents feel empowered in supporting their kids' creative endeavors, then there could be some benefit from this crisis that we have not anticipated. This may be wishful thinking on my part, but I'm trying to latch onto something positive during this bleak and uncertain time.—Pedro

---

Dear Pedro,

"Things Just Got Interesting." Love that. And a pretty good summation of this whole saga.

You've hit some key points regarding the promise and limits of remote learning. Personally, I'm growing more comfortable viewing devices and connectivity, like pencils and textbooks, as things that schools should provide to every student who needs them. That, of course, begs the question of how to most efficiently and effectively do that.

If technology is to become a regular tool for learning, this spring has raised one giant caution: Right now, at least, virtual learning is doing a lousy job of forging human connections. Teachers have reported that nearly one in four students have disappeared from their radar.[10] Surveys find students are stressed and isolated.[11] Educators, with little training in remote learning, say they're struggling to engage students. And all of this is after teachers had 6 months to bond with students before the shutdown. It has me wondering just how dismal things could get in the future if teachers are encountering students only as pixels and email accounts.

I think the biggest lesson in all of this is that online instruction cannot be jammed on top of regular routines or treated as a generic substitute for in-person teaching. I think the key to getting remote learning right, as we discussed in the context of teacher pay, is to distinguish high-value from low-value work. It's a mistake to spend class time doing things that can be done just as well remotely. If teachers only have limited time in classrooms—or in online video calls—with a student, it's vital that the time be used wisely and for things that really benefit from face-to-face intimacy.

After all, relationships are much more important for some instructional tasks than for others. Assessing a child's grasp of math operations works pretty well as an automated task. Figuring out where a kid is stuck, though, benefits immensely from direct student–teacher interaction. And, when a student is growing frustrated, in-person contact can make a huge difference.

You know, we've spoken of watching grocery clerks, janitors, truck drivers, and sanitation workers show up each day so that professionals can work comfortably from home. For me, it's a reminder that all the professionals who work in and around education—including, most assuredly, you and me—have an obligation to ensure that each of those workers can be sure their kids will enjoy the opportunities they've toiled to secure.

That's a sacred charge and a profoundly unifying one. I've spent my adult life in this work because I believe in the majesty and transformative power of education. I find myself hopeful that educators and educational leaders will rise to these challenges but unsure whether they will. With that, I'll give you the final word on this sobering subject, my friend.

Best,

Rick

Hi, Rick,

I think you've raised a tough question: What is the responsibility of teachers and schools during this difficult period? Teachers, like everyone else, are under stress. However, unlike millions of others, they are still collecting paychecks (as they should be). Now, to be fair, we must recognize that schools didn't have any time to prepare for this. One day we were getting ready for spring break. The next thing you know, school is out until next year. It was abrupt, and no one—other than the home schoolers and those who've been doing online education—was ready for this.

However, now that we know that virtual learning may become a permanent feature of education, I agree that schools must adapt to the strange and uncertain circumstances we find ourselves in. This means kids have to get more than a few packets of worksheets to do on their own. Some schools have limited instruction time to a couple hours a week. I think this is too little. My daughter gets close to 3 hours a day, and although the quality of what she gets is sometimes questionable (I can tell because I listen in and see how distracted the kids are), I appreciate that she has some structured learning time.

How will we convince the parents of kids who get much less during this period that they should support public schools when budgets get slashed—as they surely will in the weeks ahead? Los Angeles Unified School District just announced that it has a $200 million deficit.[12] As we both know, this will mean cutting staff either through mandatory furloughs or layoffs. But even as we endure the uncertainty of the pandemic, I believe we must also make sure that kids have access to learning. This might mean rethinking our priorities. Should we spend scarce resources on armed police officers or counselors and social workers? I choose the latter.

I don't want to fall into blaming teachers or schools because, as I said before, no one was prepared for this moment. Instead, I'd like to close with a thought about where education fits into America's social infrastructure. As millions of Americans become unemployed, it's becoming clear that this pandemic will trigger a depression that we are unlikely to escape quickly. Many people are already experiencing food shortages, and thousands of small businesses may never reopen. I believe that public education, like the water supply, the transportation system, police and fire departments, and so forth, must be seen as vital to the social infrastructure of society. Even when we are in a period of austerity, we never think about cutting essential services. However, schools are typically not seen in this way. This is a problem, and I think it must change if we are to have any chance of using education as a resource to secure a better future for our children.

Stay safe and healthy, my friend.—Pedro

CHAPTER 13

Closing Thoughts

As their dialogue concludes, Rick and Pedro reflect back on the months they spent in correspondence. Although far from finding consensus on major questions, and even farther from solving all that ails American education, their discussion illustrates that even those on very different sides of the ideological map can find common ground. They remind us that rage and scorn won't help us create the schools our children need. Pedro concludes that our shared future depends on our ability to reengage in civil debate. "If nothing else," he shares, he hopes readers "will appreciate our willingness to listen to each other, to take each other's ideas seriously, and when it felt right, to revise our positions based on what we have heard." Rick found their collaboration so heartening because it shows that "we can disagree on vital questions while still presuming good intentions, arguing respectfully, and extending one another a measure of grace," in a manner that "reflects the best of the American tradition." Key questions raised by these closing letters include whether it's practical to expect educators, parents, or community leaders to engage in this kind of dialogue and what it takes to seek mutual understanding or common ground.

Dear Rick,

A lot has happened in America since we started our exchange: the pandemic, a massive number of school closures as we went into quarantine, a severe economic crisis, and now the protests that are occurring throughout the country over the police and vigilante murders of Black people. We intended our exchange as an effort to communicate candidly about the controversies that have contributed to polarization in education, in an effort to see if we could find some common ground. It's for readers to decide how well we accomplished that goal. However, given what's occurred, I think it would be a mistake if we didn't attempt to make connections between recent events, as we did with the pandemic, to our exchange.

I have often said that despite their importance, educational issues are rarely seen as a priority in national politics. That may be a good thing because most politicians know very little about the complex issues facing our schools. However, at the local level, education issues are much more of a priority. I think this is the case even now. Although the media is fixated on covering the protests and clashes with police (it's hard to believe that the coronavirus is no longer the top issue in the news), parents and educators are asking for guidance on how they should speak to young people about what is happening. I've done a few webinars related to recent events and virtual learning, so I know that people are looking for guidance. There is, understandably, considerable uncertainty and concern about the state of children in America and the direction of our nation.

I believe that if we're going to make progress in addressing the issues that divide and undermine the progress of this nation—poverty, racism, inequality, and political polarization—education will have to play a central role. However, this is asking a lot of our schools and the educators who work in them. I was thinking recently: Suppose kids had been in school at the time of George Floyd's murder, a murder captured on video and seen by millions of people, including children: Would schools have known how to respond? As protests erupted and looting ensued in some cities, would educators have been able to turn this into a "teachable moment," and if so, what would they have taught?

Education is the best tool we have for transforming society, but our schools have significant limitations. We hire ordinary people to become teachers and principals but expect them to do extraordinary things. Among other things, we expect them to stimulate and challenge eager learners, to encourage and ensure evidence of learning from those who are less motivated, to support those with significant social and emotional needs, and to keep all kids safe while they are in school. Now, on top of all of that, we are expecting schools to deliver meaningful instruction to kids virtually when they had almost no time to prepare for this moment.

It's hardly surprising that so many schools fail given how much they've been asked to do. This is why I have described myself as a critical supporter of schools, especially public schools, because they are so important. No other institution, with the possible exception of police departments, is charged with meeting such a broad array of challenges. Like our police departments, our schools are often set up to fail because they lack the resources to address the complex issues they face.

This is why I believe our exchange is so important. As we know, educational issues frequently polarize our nation and many communities. Because of the polarization, we're often not able to address the difficult, complex issues that we really need to grapple with if we're going to make progress.

I welcomed the opportunity to have this exchange of views with you for three reasons:

First, I respect you. You may recall that several years ago, I chaired a search committee for a professorship at a major university (to be left unnamed) and invited you to campus. At the time, some of my colleagues were shocked. One approached me and said, "You do know that he's a conservative, don't you?" At the time, I knew very little about you. But, I had read your work, and I liked it. In my opinion, you were highly qualified and deserved to be considered. I was disappointed and a bit surprised that my liberal colleagues were so quick to dismiss you simply because of the positions you had taken on some educational issues. Although I disagree with you on several of the topics we have explored, I still respect you. I appreciate that you base your arguments on logic and facts, rather than ideology, and most of all, I appreciate your willingness to look at evidence, to listen to counterarguments as you have shown in our exchanges, and even to change your mind when you see that my points are valid.

Second, I don't believe in retreating to the comfort of our respective corners when I know there are disagreements that must be addressed. Back in 2000, I invited a conservative colleague, political scientist Jack Citrin, to engage with me in a debate over affirmative action in my classroom of 350 UC Berkeley students. Although I have strong views on the subject, I felt it was important for my students to hear from someone who would make strong, intelligent arguments so that they could make up their minds on their own. I believe debate is good and necessary for democracy.

The issues we've addressed in our letters are complex, and as such, there's plenty of room for reasonable and sincere people to disagree. I believe the current climate of polarization and the tendency to treat those we disagree with as mortal enemies prevents us from acknowledging the complexity of the issues, and in many cases from finding workable solutions. This is not an argument for compromise simply for the sake of avoiding an argument. Like you, I'm always willing to participate in an intelligent debate, and I'm definitely willing to fight for the things I believe in.

However, I reject the idea of villainizing people who disagree with me simply because we don't see things the same way on every educational issue. I am not the type who is satisfied speaking or writing exclusively to people who already agree with me. I'm so confident about some of my views that I'm willing to readily engage and attempt to persuade those who disagree with me. That's why I welcome the opportunity to speak to educators and policymakers in red states, and even before potentially hostile audiences.

For example, a few years ago, I wrote an op-ed for the *Wall Street Journal* about *Vergara v. California.*[1] As you will recall, this was a case that called for the elimination of tenure for teachers based on the idea that tenure was making it possible for incompetent teachers to retain their jobs in schools serving disadvantaged kids. In the editorial, I agreed that there were ineffective teachers who should be removed (with due process) from teaching, but I argued that retaining teacher tenure was important for making a tough job attractive. I also argued that blaming teachers for the poor performance of some schools was unfair and similar to blaming doctors and nurses at underresourced Veterans Affairs hospitals for poor quality of service. In response to my editorial, the superintendent of a major school district left me an abusive voicemail message. Because I regarded him as a friend, I called him and asked if he would like to discuss our different perspectives on the issue. To this day, we have never had a conversation about our disagreement. I consider his unwillingness to engage in a dialogue over our disagreement an unfortunate lack of maturity on his part. However, I realize that his response has become an increasingly common way of dealing with political differences in this country.

This leads me to my final point. Our country needs to learn how to engage in civil debate. If nothing else, I hope that those who read our book will appreciate our willingness to listen to each other, to take each other's ideas seriously, and when it felt right, to revise our positions based on what we have heard.

This seems to matter now more than ever. I have been participating in protests over the last few days. In fact, last Saturday, I participated in three in a single day. I brought my wife and 8-year-old daughter along. Initially, my daughter was scared to go. She was worried that we would be teargased and beaten by riot police. I told her that was why we had to go, because protesting was the only weapon we had available for asserting our right to freedom of speech and assembly.

Since the protests, I've been listening to the debates about policing and watching how politicians respond to calls for defunding the police. I have a lot of feelings about this issue, in part because my father was a police officer in New York City for 23 years. He retired after he was injured in the line of duty and became permanently disabled after attempting to intervene in a fight between another officer and a man who had been involved in a domestic dispute. My father practiced community policing before it was called by that name. He knew the residents of the neighborhoods he patrolled, and they trusted him. Many of them invited him to their home for meals, after work, of course. He took pride in the fact that he never shot anyone and never had a complaint filed against him. This was New York City in the 1960s and 1970s, a much rougher place than it is today.

I have also been victimized by the police. The last time it occurred was when I was still living in New York City. I was stopped and frisked by the police after speaking at an event in the Bronx on school safety with the New York City Schools chancellor. Initially, I questioned why they stopped me and refused to tell them where I worked after I had given them my driver's license because I felt it was an unfair question. I only agreed to be more cooperative when I realized that they might arrest me. I was incensed by the harassment, but I knew it was part of a strategy that had been famously embraced by Mayor Mike Bloomberg in the name of safety. I knew that I had only been stopped because I was a Black man, guilty of the crime of walking while Black.

These are the types of indignities that Black people endure on a regular basis in this country. Most of the time these encounters are not captured on camera, and like the tree that falls in the forest with no one around to hear, if it's not caught on camera, it can be easily denied by the perpetrating officers.

This is the world that our kids and the kids we've been writing about are being prepared for. Will they accept injustice and racism as simply an unfortunate aspect of life, or will they strenuously object even when they are not directly affected? Will they tolerate the growing number of people living on our streets and languishing in our prisons or aspire and strive to create a society that is more just and compassionate?

I believe that education must prepare children to actively participate in democracy and answer questions such as these; otherwise, our democracy will be imperiled. They must learn that democracy requires more of us than voting. For democracy to thrive, we must hold our leaders and public institutions accountable, engage and interact with our neighbors, fight against injustice, and look out for those who are most vulnerable.

So, in a small way, I hope that this exchange is helpful to our democracy. Education may not be the most important issue facing this country, but I believe it is the best resource we have to create a more just and equitable future.

I wish you well, my friend.—Pedro

Dear Pedro,

When we started this correspondence, I imagined it playing out differently than it has. Although we'd said it should be a search for understanding, I'm pretty sure I expected more of a debate. That's not because I thought the world needed one more debate right now or because we'd settle anything—it's just what I've grown used to. I love that it turned into something else entirely: an actual dialogue where we found a surprising amount of common ground along the way.

I, too, still remember when you invited me for that campus job talk two decades ago. I remember being honored that you were interested in what I had to say. I'm also moved to report, though, that I've found that kind of intellectual curiosity more the exception than the rule in our work.

When it comes to the tough issues we've explored—from privatization to diversity—there's a lot of huddling with fellow believers and deploring those who see things differently. Over the years, I haven't seen nearly as much serious discussion across the divides as I might've hoped. The discourse is too often dominated by table-pounding champions who insist that their side is "for the children" and that those who disagree with their prescriptions are selfish, ignorant, and, presumably, anti-child.

Deviations from the party line can anger friends, alienate allies, and cause foundations to stop answering email. And it needn't take too many departures from orthodoxy to smother a career or leave an iconoclast isolated and adrift. This results in a dearth of reflection and little room for serious dialogue.

All this is so prevalent, I suspect, because education (like politics) is a magnet for passionate people. This can be a great blessing. It can also be a curse. Passion doesn't necessarily coexist with humility, curiosity, or deliberation. Indeed, in a polarized, hot-take era, passion can fuel division and distrust.

This spring, during the slow days of the coronavirus lockdown, I found myself searching my shelves for a volume with Yeats's "The Second Coming."[2] The poem had been on my mind, and I'd been reflecting on its iconic lament:

> Things fall apart; the centre cannot hold;
> Mere anarchy is loosed upon the world . . .
> The best lack all conviction, while the worst
> Are full of passionate intensity.

There's a fierce need in the current age, I think, for people of conviction to help the center hold. Otherwise, the flood of passionate intensity threatens to tear us apart. Channeling that passion into constructive change requires leaders who are willing to speak deliberately, reason with opponents, and work within institutions. Absent that leadership, passion can too easily follow the path of least resistance, fueling frustration, division, and destruction.

A crumbling moral center has grave costs. It means there are too few able or willing to reach across the chasm to cultivate trust and forge workable solutions. And because so many institutions and habits that once helped bridge our divides have atrophied, we need to build new ones.

I think that's why I've found this exercise so powerful. Although I've had more than my share of extended conversations with Left-leaning colleagues, those tend to be much less instructive than this has been. After all, when you're face-to-face in an energetic back-and-forth, there's not a lot of time to reflect. It's easy to get more caught up in rebutting a point than absorbing it.

Our correspondence offered something different. It forced us to stay with uncomfortable topics even when one of us might've preferred to move on. It allowed us to reflect and not just respond. We couldn't simply settle for whatever quick quip or reflexive riposte leapt to mind. The opportunity to sit down, read your take, consider it, and then collect my own thoughts before responding, and to do this time and again over an extended period, has made for an all-too-uncommon experience.

From one letter to the next, I could actually feel my trust growing. And I think the willingness to be transparent and open grew in turn. That may help explain why so many of your insights registered with me and why we found so many points of unexpected agreement.

Recalling your riff on the underrated importance of supporting school leaders brings a wry grin. As that principal put it to you, "If you can't stop a food fight, you shouldn't be a principal." Your anecdote perfectly nails the fantasy that some magical pedagogy or program will make up for a lack of professional skill or discipline. When you quoted your dad pointing out that a library card was a ticket to an education, it brought a practical lens to an esoteric discussion about educational purpose. When we talked privatization, I loved your evocation of New York City's subways, of that vision of all New Yorkers, rich and poor, bankers and bodega workers alike, riding together. It was a powerful reminder that our efforts to improve schooling should always be grounded in an appreciation of how students, families, and communities experience their schools.

On the larger questions, we disagreed pretty resolutely in some predictable places, as when it came to school choice, for-profits, and big philanthropy. Yet we stumbled across some substantial points of agreement on certain big issues. Although testing and accountability sparked some of the fiercest education debates of the past two decades, we seemed to find broad agreement on many key points. I think we agreed that assessments are valuable but overused, that accountability bit off more than it could chew, that it's crucial to measure more than reading and math scores, and that testing should place more emphasis on learning and less on labeling schools and teachers.

We had interesting differences on school funding but seemed to be pretty close when it came to teacher pay, agreeing that there's a strong case for paying teachers more, that teacher roles should be rethought in concert with heightened pay, that benefits need to be adjusted, that tenure should be extended, and that there's a need to rethink the role of support staff.

This all brings to mind a striking report by the nonprofit Beyond Conflict. In our introduction, we mentioned a 2019 report on the hyperpolarization of political activists. Well, this summer, Beyond Conflict reported the surprising fact that our political opponents generally have a higher opinion of us than we imagine.[3] On both the Left and the Right, we think those on the other side deem us deplorable and respond in kind. In reality, though, their views turn out to be much more charitable than we think.

As former secretary of defense James Mattis, perhaps the nation's greatest living general, put it so aptly this summer:

> We practice suspicion or contempt where trust is needed. . . . We scorch our opponents with language that precludes compromise. We brush aside the possibility that a person with whom we disagree might be right. We talk about what divides us and seldom acknowledge what unites us.[4]

The way out of this destructive spiral, I suspect, is a version of what you and I have done here. Our conversation showed me that we have more in common than I'd realized and that we can disagree on vital questions while still presuming good intentions, arguing respectfully, and extending one another a measure of grace.

You made me think and wonder, my friend. Thank you. The whole experience was both disconcertingly unusual and unusually rewarding.

I'm left wondering how we might foster more of this kind of conversation. I've been musing on what made this work. For starters, we knew, liked, and trusted each other. Our work certainly gives us the time to engage in something like this. We got away from the now familiar habit of policing one another's statements with an eye to scoring points or finding cause to take offense. I'm sure I used turns of phrase that rubbed you wrong, but you were always willing to engage over the substance and deal in good faith. I tried to do the same.

And we didn't engage in the popular game of "what-aboutism." So many debates today are consumed with those on one side asking those on the other, "What about X?"—demanding endless explanations as to why they didn't say this or denounce that. You and I were blessedly able to resist treating ellipses as signs of hidden agendas. Moreover, once we'd made a point or clarified a disagreement, we were able to move on without rancor. That created room for exploration to continue and for agreement to take root.

As our little journey draws to a close, I find myself satisfied but also wistful. We did something difficult at a time when it feels exceptionally important. Indeed, we did something that reflects the best of the American tradition. This nation is a great and remarkable project. But, ultimately, this grand project is only what we make of it.

In early 2020, my former boss Arthur Brooks, now comfortably ensconced up at Harvard University, delivered a keynote at the annual National Prayer Breakfast.[5] Arthur's theme was the need to love our enemies. He put it thusly, "As the Rev. Martin Luther King Jr. taught about the verse on which my speech was based, 'If you hate your enemies, you have no way to redeem and to transform your enemies.'" He was immediately followed by President Donald Trump, who summarily dismissed Arthur's message as a naive critique of his combative leadership style.

I thought Arthur's reflection on the experience captured so much of what is best about America and about the spirit that's animated our correspondence. In the *Washington Post,* he wrote:

> I spoke my mind, and the president of the United States listened to me. Then, the president spoke his mind, and I listened to him. We obviously do not see the treatment of our political foes in the same way. I think I am right; he thinks he is right. After the event, I went about my day without incident (beyond the predictable toxic bilge on social media, which is

meaningless). I went home to Boston, slept well, and got up to find that I still had a job at my university.

President Trump and I gave quite different speeches at the National Prayer Breakfast, that is true. But there was one point on which we agreed completely. It was the last line in each of our speeches: "God bless America." I know the phrase sounds like a cliché, but it isn't to me.

I disagreed, on national television, with the most powerful person in the world. It was no problem. God bless America.[6]

You know, when I started teaching high school in East Baton Rouge Parish all those years ago, I had a vague notion that education would be a place where that blessing was steadfastly embraced. I imagined that those attracted to our field would be inquisitive and curious, that we would challenge our assumptions and learn from one another.

That has been true far less often than I had hoped. But this exercise has reaffirmed my faith. It has strengthened my conviction that we can rise to the challenge, that we can bind our wounds and summon the better angels of our nature. After all, we've done it so very many times before.

Best,
Rick

Notes

Preface

1. Baldwin, J. (2019, February 2). *Black History Month* [blog]. www.thebeeand thefox.com/blogs/news/black-history-month-james-baldwin.

Chapter 1

1. Sunstein, C. (1999, December 13). *The law of group polarization* (Doctoral dissertation, University of Chicago Law School, John M. Olin Law & Economics Working Paper No. 91 [Abstract]). https://papers.ssrn.com/sol3/papers.cfm ?abstract_id=199668.

2. Fleisher, L. (2012, February 2). SUNY official resigns over charter issue. *Wall Street Journal*. www.wsj.com/articles/SB10001424052970204652904577197 550308368954.

3. Newseditor. (n.d.). *Q&A on common sense school reform*. www.gse.harvard .edu/news/ed/04/08/qa-common-sense-school-reform.

4. Noguera, P. (2013, August 7). *Federal role in education is to protect vulnerable students*. The American Way of Learning [blog]. www.nytimes.com/room fordebate/2012/12/10/the-american-way-of-learning/federal-role-in-education -is-to-protect-vulnerable-students; Hess, F. M. (2012, December 11). *Enforcing Common Core standards would be risky*. The American Way of Learning [blog]. www.nytimes.com/roomfordebate/2012/12/10/the-american-way-of-learning /enforcing-common-core-standards-would-be-risky.

5. Strauss, V. (2012, May 16). Why education inequality persists—and how to fix it. *Washington Post*. https://www.washingtonpost.com/blogs/answer-sheet/post /why-education-inequality-persists--and-how-to-fix-it/2012/05/15/gIQAXEIeSU _blog.html; Hess, F. M., & Cummings, A. (2017, September 26). The funding crisis myth. *U.S. News & World Report*. https://www.usnews.com/opinion/knowledge -bank/articles/2017-09-26/the-problem-with-worrying-that-us-schools-face-an -education-funding-crisis.

6. Hess, F. M. (2014, June 11). No shortcut to school reform: Column. *USA Today*. https://www.usatoday.com/story/opinion/2014/06/11/school-reform-vergara -california-teacher-tenure-column/10321765/; Noguera, P. (2014, June 18). In de-

fense of teacher tenure. *Wall Street Journal.* https://www.wsj.com/articles/pedro
-noguera-in-defense-of-teacher-tenure-1403134951.

7. Edsall, T. B. (2019, March 13). No hate left behind. *New York Times.* https://
www.nytimes.com/2019/03/13/opinion/hate-politics.html.

8. More in Common. *The perception gap.* (2019). https://perceptiongap.us.

9. Balz, D. (2019, October 26). Americans hate all the partisanship, but
they're also more partisan than they were. *Washington Post.* https://www
.washingtonpost.com/politics/americans-hate-all-the-partisanship-but-theyre
-also-more-partisan-than-they-were/2019/10/26/e1f4abe2-f762-11e9-a285
-882a8e386a96_story.html.

10. National Historical Publications and Records Commission (Ed.). (n.d.). *Founders Online: John Adams to Thomas Jefferson, 15 July 1813, with postscript* . . . (n.d.).
https://www.founders.archives.gov/documents/Jefferson/03-06-02-0247.

Chapter 2

1. Lutz, A. (2008). Who joins the military? A look at race, class, and immigration status. *Journal of Political and Military Sociology, 36*(2), 167–188. https://
surface.syr.edu/cgi/viewcontent.cgi?article=1002&context=soc.

2. Rush, B. (1986). Benjamin Rush, Of the mode of education proper in a
republic. In P. B. Kurland & R. Lerner (Eds.), *The Founder's Constitution* (Vol. 1,
p. 686). The University of Chicago Press. https://press-pubs.uchicago.edu/founders
/documents/v1ch18s30.html (original work published 1798).

3. Aristotle. (n.d.). Forbes Quotes. www.forbes.com/quotes/657.

4. Strauss, V. (2020, April 27). Teachers, parents and principals tell their stories about remote learning. *Washington Post.* www.washingtonpost.com/education
/2020/04/27/teachers-parents-principals-tell-their-stories-about-remote-learning.

5. McKenna, L. (2012). The big idea that can revolutionize higher education:
"MOOC." *The Atlantic.* www.theatlantic.com/business/archive/2012/05/the-big-idea
-that-can-revolutionize-higher-education-mooc/256926.

6. Reich, J., & Ruipérez-Valiente, J. A. (2019). The MOOC pivot. *Science,
363*(6423), 130–131. doi:10.1126/science.aav7958.

Chapter 3

1. Libetti, A., Burgoyne-Allen, P., Lewis, B., & Schmitz, K. (2019, January 22).
The state of the charter sector. www.bellwethereducation.org/publication/state
-charter-sector; Rhinesmith, E. (2017). A review of the research on parent satisfac-
tion in private school choice programs. *Journal of School Choice, 11*(4), 585–603.
doi:10.1080/15582159.2017.1395639.

2. Burris, C., & Pfleger, R. (2020). *Broken promises: An analysis of charter
school closures from 1999–2017.* Network for Public Education. www.networkfor
publiceducation.org/brokenpromises.

3. Gross, B., & Lake, R. (2014). *Special education in charter schools: What we've learned and what we still need to know.* Center on Reinventing Public Education. www.crpe.org/sites/default/files/crpe-special-education-in-charter-schools-what-learned-what-we-still-need-to-know.pdf.

4. Gross, B., & Lake, R. (2014, December). *Special education in charter schools: What we've learned and what we still need to know.* Center on Reinventing Public Education. www.crpe.org/sites/default/files/crpe-special-education-in-charter-schools-what-learned-what-we-still-need-to-know.pdf.

5. Artiles, A. J., Harry, B., Reschly, D. J., & Chinn, P. C. (2002). Over-identification of students of color in special education: A critical overview. *Multicultural Perspectives, 4*(1), 3–10. doi:10.1207/s15327892mcp0401_2.

6. Success Academy Charter Schools. (2019). *Our 2019 results.* Retrieved August 6, 2020, from www.successacademies.org/results.

7. Pondiscio, R. (2019). *How the other half learns: Equality, excellence, and the battle over school choice.* Avery.

8. Pondiscio, R. (2020, May 20). *On distance learning, Success Academy once again leads the way.* Retrieved August 6, 2020, from www.fordhaminstitute.org/national/commentary/distance-learning-success-academy-once-again-leads-way.

9. Bedrick, J., & Burke, L. (2018, October 30). *Surveying Florida scholarship families* (Rep.). www.edchoice.org/research/surveying-florida-scholarship-families.

10. Scafidi, B. (2012, February 29). *The fiscal effects of school choice programs on public school districts.* The Friedman Foundation for Educational Choice. www.edchoice.org/research/the-fiscal-effects-of-school-choice-programs-on-public-school-districts; Fullerton, J., & Roza, M. (2016, March 03). *Funding phantom students.* Retrieved September 1, 2020, from https://www.educationnext.org/funding-phantom-students.

11. Figlio, D. N., & Hart, C. M. (2010, June). *Competitive effects of means-tested school vouchers* (Working paper No. 16056). National Bureau of Economic Research. www.nber.org/papers/w16056.

12. *Over the counter, under the radar: Inequitably distributing New York City's late-enrolling high school students.* (2013). Annenberg Institute. www.annenberginstitute.org/publications/over-counter-under-radar-inequitably-distributing-new-york-citys-late-enrolling-high.

13. The Parthenon Group. *NYC secondary reform selected analysis.* (2011). https://www.classsizematters.org/wp-content/uploads/2013/05/parthenon-2006.pdf.

14. Brint, S. (2017). *Schools and societies.* Stanford University Press.

Chapter 4

1. Goluboff, R. (2020, May 30). *Brown v. board of education.* Miller Center. Retrieved July 22, 2020, from www.millercenter.org/the-presidency/educational-resources/brown-v-board-education.

2. Orfield, G. (2016, May 23). *"Brown" at 62: School segregation by race, poverty and state*. Civil Rights Project. https://eric.ed.gov/?id=ED565900.

3. U.S. Department of Education Office for Civil Rights. (2014, March). *Civil Rights Data Collection, Data Snapshot: Early childhood education*. www2.ed.gov /about/offices/list/ocr/docs/crdc-early-learning-snapshot.pdf.

4. U.S. Department of Education, Office for Civil Rights Delivering Justice, Under Section 203(b)(1) of the Department of Education Organization Act, FY 2015, Washington, D.C., 2016.

5. Institute of Education Sciences. (2016). *Public school students eligible for free or reduced-price lunch*. www.nces.ed.gov/fastfacts/display.asp?id=898; National Center for Children in Poverty. (n.d.). *Child poverty*. www.nccp.org /demographic/?state=US.

6. U.S. Commission on Civil Rights. (2018, January 10). *Public education funding inequity in an era of increasing concentration of poverty and resegregation*. www.usccr.gov/pubs/2018/2018-01-10-Education-Inequity.pdf.

7. For a more extended treatment of this idea, see Hess, F. M., & Addison, J. G. (2019). Busting the college-industrial complex. *National Affairs, 40*. www .nationalaffairs.com/publications/detail/busting-the-college-industrial-complex.

8. Kramer, S. (2019, December 12). *U.S. has world's highest rate of children living in single-parent households*. www.pewresearch.org/fact-tank/2019/12/12/u -s-children-more-likely-than-children-in-other-countries-to-live-with-just-one -parent.

9. Ziol-Guest, K. M., Duncan, G. J., & Kalil, A. (2015). One-parent students leave school earlier. *Education Next, 15*(2). www.educationnext.org/one-parent -students-leave-school-earlier.

10. Barrett, N., McEachin, A., Mills, J. N., & Valant, J. (2017, November 20). *What are the sources of school discipline disparities by student race and family income?* Education Research Alliance for New Orleans. https://education researchalliancenola.org/publications/what-are-the-sources-of-school-discipline -disparities-by-student-race-and-family-income.

11. Haskins, R., & Sawhill, I. V. (2009). *Creating an opportunity society*. Brookings Institution Press.

12. Garbacz, S. A., Herman, K. C., Thompson, A. M., & Reinke, W. M. (2017). Family engagement in education and intervention: Implementation and evaluation to maximize family, school, and student outcomes. *Journal of School Psychology, 62,* 1–10. doi:10.1016/j.jsp.2017.04.00.

13. An, S. (2019, July 25). *Hundreds of school districts nationally deeply divided based on race and funding*. National Public Radio. www.npr.org/local/309 /2019/07/25/745201598/hundreds-of-school-districts-nationally-deeply-divided -based-on-race-and-funding.

14. The Educational Opportunity Monitoring Project. (n.d.). *Racial and ethnic achievement gaps*. Center for Education Policy Analysis, Stanford University. https://

cepa.stanford.edu/educational-opportunity-monitoring-project/achievement-gaps
/race.

15. Camera, L. (2019, March 4). Teachers union launches national education-funding campaign. *U.S. News & World Report.* www.usnews.com/news/education
-news/articles/2019-03-04/teachers-union-launches-national-education-funding
-campaign.

16. Eden, M. (2019, July 25). *Issues 2020: Public school spending is at an all-time high.* Retrieved August 27, 2020, from www.manhattan-institute.org/issues
-2020-us-public-school-spending-teachers-pay.

17. Rueben, K., & Murray, S. (2008). *Racial disparities in education finance: Going beyond equal revenues.* Tax Policy Center. www.taxpolicycenter.org/publications
/racial-disparities-education-finance-going-beyond-equal-revenues/full.

18. Chingos, M., & Blagg, K. (2017, June 1). *Do poor kids get their fair share of school funding?* The Urban Institute. www.urban.org/research/publication/do
-poor-kids-get-their-fair-share-school-funding.

19. Clark, A., & Raychaudhuri, D. (2019, August 20). *Here's what every N.J. district spends per student.* www.nj.com/education/2019/08/heres-what-every-nj
-district-spends-per-student.html.

20. Amin, R. (2020, January 27). *NYC spends a record $28K per student, but the state is footing a smaller portion of that bill.* Retrieved August 6, 2020, from https://ny.chalkbeat.org/2020/1/27/21121084/nyc-spends-a-record-28k-per
-student-but-the-state-is-footing-a-smaller-portion-of-that-bill; Board, P. (2020, May 18). Carranza's "cut to the bone" schools budget still packed with central-office fat [Editorial]. *New York Post.* www.nypost.com/2020/05/18/carranzas-schools
-budget-still-packed-with-central-office-fat.

21. Los Angeles Unified School District. (2017, August). *Health and welfare board retreat.* Retrieved from https://boe.lausd.net/sites/default/files/08-29-17Hea
lthandWelfarePresentationFinal_0.pdf.

22. Schwalbach, J., & Burke, L. (2018, May 1). *High public school spending in DC hasn't produced desired outcomes* [Commentary]. Retrieved August 6, 2020, from www.heritage.org/education/commentary/high-public-school-spending-dc
-hasnt-produced-desired-outcomes.

23. U.S. Commission on Civil Rights. (2018, January 10). *Public education funding inequity in an era of increasing concentration of poverty and resegregation.* from www.usccr.gov/pubs/2018/2018-01-10-Education-Inequity.pdf.

24. Kincheloe, J. L. (2010). Why a book on urban education? In S. Steinberg (Ed.), *19 urban questions: Teaching in the city* (2nd ed., pp. 1–28). Peter Lang Publishing.

25. Brint, S. (2017). *Schools and societies.* Stanford University Press.

Chapter 5

1. Noguera, P., Bishop, J. Howard, T., & Johnson, S. (2019). *Beyond the schoolhouse: Overcoming challenges & expanding opportunities for Black youth in Los*

Angeles County. Center for the Transformation of Schools, Black Male Institute, Graduate School of Education & Information Studies, University of California, Los Angeles.

2. Hess, F. (2003). The case for being mean. *Educational Leadership: The Challenges of Accountability, 61*(3), 22–26. www.ascd.org/publications/educational-leadership/nov03/vol61/num03/The-Case-for-Being-Mean.aspx.

3. Hess, F. M. (2008/2009, December/January). The new stupid. *Educational Leadership: The Challenges of Accountability, 66*(4), 12–17. http://www.ascd.org/publications/educational-leadership/dec08/vol66/num04/The-New-Stupid.aspx.

4. UC Academic Council's Standardized Testing Task Force. (2020). *Report of the UC academic council standardized testing task force (STTF)*. University of California. https://senate.universityofcalifornia.edu/_files/underreview/sttf-report.pdf.

5. Jaschik, S. (2017, July 17). *High school grades: Higher and higher.* Inside Higher Ed. www.insidehighered.com/admissions/article/2017/07/17/study-finds-notable-increase-grades-high-schools-nationally.

6. Lemann, P. N. (2000). *The big test: The secret history of the American meritocracy.* Farrar, Straus and Giroux.

7. Koretz, D., McCaffery, D., Klein, S., Bell, R., & Stecher, B. (1992). *The reliability of scores from the 1992 Vermont portfolio assessment program* (pp. 1–28). RAND Corporation. www.rand.org/pubs/drafts/DRU159.html.

8. Fullan, M., & Quinn, J. (2015). *Coherence: The right drivers in action for schools, districts, and systems.* Corwin Press.

9. Schueler, B. E. (2019). A third way: The politics of school district takeover and turnaround in Lawrence, Massachusetts. *Educational Administration Quarterly, 55*(1), 116–153. doi:10.1177/0013161X18785873.

10. Hart, R., Casserly, M., Uzzell, R., Palacios, M., Corcoran, A., & Spurgeon, L. (2015, October). *Student testing in America's great city schools: An inventory and preliminary analysis* (Rep.). Council of the Great City Schools. www.cgcs.org/cms/lib/DC00001581/Centricity/Domain/87/Testing%20Report.pdf.

11. U.S. Bureau of Labor Statistics. (2016, April 28). *Entrepreneurship and the U.S. economy.* www.bls.gov/bdm/entrepreneurship/entrepreneurship.htm.

Chapter 6

1. Devitt, M. (2019, March 18). *Study: One in six U.S. children has a mental illness.* Retrieved August 6, 2020, from www.aafp.org/news/health-of-the-public/20190318childmentalillness.html.

2. Hedegaard, H., Curtin, S., & Warner, M., *Increase in suicide mortality in the United States, 1999–2018.* (2020, April). CDC. https://pubmed.ncbi.nlm.nih.gov/32487287/; Graf, N. (2018, April 18). *Majority of teens worry about school shootings, and so do most parents.* Pew Research Center. www.pewresearch.org/fact-tank/2018/04/18/a-majority-of-u-s-teens-fear-a-shooting-could-happen-at-their-school-and-most-parents-share-their-concern.

3. Rhames, M. A. (2019, July 23). *The "f-word" of social-emotional learning: Faith*. American Enterprise Institute. Retrieved August 26, 2020, from www.aei.org /research-products/report/the-f-word-of-social-and-emotional-learning-faith.

4. Mcleod, S. (2013). *Kohlberg's stages of moral development*. Simply Psychology. www.simplypsychology.org/kohlberg.html.

5. Huntsberry, W. (2020, March 2). *One City Heights school is doing the nearly impossible: Closing the achievement gap*. www.voiceofsandiego.org/topics /education/one-city-heights-school-is-doing-the-nearly-impossible-closing-the -achievement-gap.

Chapter 7

1. Annenberg Public Policy Center. (2016, September 13). *Americans' knowledge of the branches of government is declining*. www.annenbergpublicpolicycenter .org/americans-knowledge-of-the-branches-of-the-government-is-declining.

2. The Woodrow Wilson National Fellowship Foundation. (2018, October 3). *National survey finds just 1 in 3 Americans would pass citizenship test*. www .woodrow.org/news/national-survey-finds-just-1-in-3-americans-would-pass -citizenship-test.

3. Grabar, M. (2019). *Debunking Howard Zinn: Exposing the fake history that turned a generation against America*. Regnery History.

4. Kaufman, E. (2019, December 16). The "1619 Project" gets schooled. *Wall Street Journal*. www.wsj.com/articles/the-1619-project-gets-schooled-11576540494; Silverstein, J. (2019, December 20). We respond to the historians who critiqued the 1619 Project. *New York Times*. www.nytimes.com/2019/12/20/magazine/we -respond-to-the-historians-who-critiqued-the-1619-project.html.

5. Zinn, H. (1980). *A people's history of the United States*. Harper.

6. Petrilli, M. J., & Finn, C. E. (2020). *How to educate an American: The conservative vision for tomorrow's schools*. Templeton Press.

7. Lewis, J. (2020, July 30). Together, you can redeem the soul of our nation. *New York Times*. www.nytimes.com/2020/07/30/opinion/john-lewis-civil-rights -america.html.

8. Blakemore, E. (2017, October 11). *Did George Washington really free Mount Vernon's enslaved workers?* www.history.com/news/did-george-washington-really -free-mount-vernons-slaves.

9. Thomas Jefferson Foundation. (n.d.). If we are to guard against ignorance ... (Spurious Quotation). www.monticello.org/site/research-and-collections /if-we-are-guard-against-ignorance-spurious-quotation.

10. The Avalon Project. (2008). *Thomas Jefferson first inaugural address*. https://avalon.law.yale.edu/19th_century/jefinau1.asp.

11. Hess, F. M., & Addison, G. (2017, October 2). Betsy DeVos vs. the mindless mob at Harvard. *National Review*. www.nationalreview.com/2017/10/betsy-devos -harvard-speech-education-secretary-campus-protest-free-speech-school-choice.

Chapter 8

1. 20th Century Fox. (1987). *The Princess Bride.*

2. Ni, Y. (2012). Teacher working conditions in charter schools and traditional public schools: A comparative study. *Teachers College Record, 114*(3), 1–26. www.researchgate.net/publication/297452024_Teacher_Working_Conditions_in _Charter_Schools_and_Traditional_Public_Schools_A_Comparative_Study.

3. Torre, K. (2013). Charter schools and the process of "counseling out." *Theory, Research, and Action in Urban Education, 2*(1). https://traue.commons.gc .cuny.edu/issue-2-fall-2013/torre.

4. Rosenberg, S., & Silva, E. (2012). *Trending toward reform: Teachers speak on unions and the future of the profession* (Rep.). Washington, D.C.: Education Sector. (ERIC Document Reproduction Service No. ED533492).

5. Murnana, R. J., Mbeakeani, P. P., Reardon, S. F., & Lamb, A. (2018, July 17). Who goes to private school? *Education Next, 18*(4). www.educationnext.org/who -goes-private-school-long-term-enrollment-trends-family-income.

6. Goodnough, A. (2020, August 14). Families priced out of "learning pods" seek alternatives. *New York Times.* www.nytimes.com/2020/08/14/us/covid-schools -learning-pods.html.

Chapter 9

1. Strauss, V. (2014, June 9). How much Bill Gates's disappointing small-schools effort really cost. *Washington Post.* www.washingtonpost.com/news/answer-sheet /wp/2014/06/09/how-much-bill-gatess-disappointing-small-schools-effort-really -cost.

2. Siegel, B., & Kim, S. R. (2020, April 20). Mike Bloomberg spent more than $1 billion on four-month presidential campaign according to filing. *ABC News.* www.abcnews.go.com/Politics/mike-bloomberg-spent-billion-month-presidential -campaign-filing/story?id=70252435; *New York Times.* (2012). The 2012 money race: Compare the candidates. www.nytimes.com/elections/2012/campaign-finance .html.

3. Blume, H. (2017, August 3). Late donations from Eli Broad and others helped charter advocates shift power on L.A. school board. *Los Angeles Times.* www.latimes .com/local/lanow/la-me-edu-la-school-board-money-20170803-story.html.

4. Madrigal, A. C. (2018, June 27). Against big philanthropy. *The Atlantic.* www.theatlantic.com/technology/archive/2018/06/against-philanthropy/563834.

5. See, for instance, Hess, F. M. (2005). *With the best of intentions: How philanthropy is reshaping K–12 education.* Harvard Education Press; Hess, F. M., & Henig, J. R. (Eds.). (2015). *The new education philanthropy: Politics, policy, and reform.* Harvard Education Press.

6. Hess, F. M. (2020, January 17). *The 2020 RHSU edu-scholar public influence rankings.* https://blogs.edweek.org/edweek/rick_hess_straight_up/2020/01 /the_2020_rhsu-edu-scholar_public_influence_rankings.html.

7. Zinsmeister, K. (n.d.). Who gives most to charity? In *The Almanac of American Philanthropy*. Philanthropy Roundtable. www.philanthropyroundtable.org /almanac/statistics/who-gives.

8. Stecher, B. M., Holtzman, D. J., Garet, M. S., Hamilton, L. S., Engberg, J., Steiner, E. D., Robyn, A., Baird, M., I. A., Guitierrez, E. D., Peet, Brodziak de los Reyes, I., Fronberg, K., Weinberger, G., Hunter, G. P., & Chambers, J. (2018). *Improving teaching effectiveness: Final report* (Rep.). RAND Corporation. www.rand .org/pubs/research_reports/RR2242.html.

Chapter 10

1. Orfield, G., Frankenberg, E., Ee, J., & Kuscera, J. (2014, May 15). *Brown at 60: Great progress, a long retreat and an uncertain future.* The Civil Rights Project. www.civilrightsproject.ucla.edu/research/k-12-education/integration-and -diversity/brown-at-60-great-progress-a-long-retreat-and-an-uncertain-future.

2. Urban Institute. (2020). *Segregated neighborhoods, segregated schools?* www.urban.org/features/segregated-neighborhoods-segregated-schools.

3. Lockhart, P. (2019, May 10). *65 years after* Brown v. Board of Education, *school segregation is getting worse.* Vox. www.vox.com/identities/2019/5/10 /18566052/school-segregation-brown-board-education-report.

4. Orfield, G., Ee, J., Frankenberg, E., & Siegel-Hawley, G. (2016). *Brown at 62: School segregation by race, poverty, and state* (pp. 1–9). Civil Rights Project, UCLA. www.civilrightsproject.ucla.edu.

5. Frey, W. H. (2019). *Less than half of US children under 15 are white, census shows.* Brookings Institution. www.brookings.edu/research/less-than-half-of-us -children-under-15-are-white-census-shows.

6. Geiger, A. (2017, October 25). *Many minority kids go to schools where at least half of students are their race, ethnicity.* Pew Research. www.pewresearch .org/fact-tank/2017/10/25/many-minority-students-go-to-schools-where-at-least -half-of-their-peers-are-their-race-or-ethnicity.

7. Data USA. (2020). *Vermont.* Retrieved August 29, 2020, from www.datausa .io/profile/geo/vermont.

8. Haskins, R., Isaacs, J. B., & Sawhill, I. V. (2008). *Getting ahead or losing ground: Economic mobility in America.* Brookings Institution Press. www.brookings .edu/research/getting-ahead-or-losing-ground-economic-mobility-in-america.

9. Barth, R. (2020, July 1). *Richard Barth's Weekly Thoughts: Turning words into action.* KIPP Public Charter Schools. www.kipp.org/news/weekly-thoughts -turning-words-into-action.

10. Italiano, L. (2020, July 16). "Whiteness" exhibit at Smithsonian's African American History Museum causes stir. *New York Post.* www.nypost.com/2020/07 /16/african-american-history-museums-whiteness-exhibit-raising-eyebrows.

11. Harvey, R. S. (2020, August 17). An open letter to well-meaning white teachers. *Education Week.* www.edweek.org/ew/articles/2020/08/17/an-open-letter -to-well-meaning-white-teachers.html?cmp=eml-enl-eu-news2.

12. NCES. (2020, May). Characteristics of public school teachers. *The Condition of Education* [blog]. Retrieved September 3, 2020, from www.nces.ed.gov/programs/coe/indicator_clr.asp.

13. Chen, G. (2019, October 14). White students are now the minority in U.S. public schools. *About Public Schools* [blog]. www.publicschoolreview.com/blog/white-students-are-now-the-minority-in-u-s-public-schools.

14. National Center for Science and Engineering Statistics. (2019). *Women, minorities, and persons with disabilities in science and engineering.* National Science Foundation. www.ncses.nsf.gov/pubs/nsf19304/digest/about-this-report.

15. Hrabowski, F. A., III, & Henderson, P. H. (2019, November 29). How to actually promote diversity in STEM. *The Atlantic.* www.theatlantic.com/ideas/archive/2019/11/how-umbc-got-minority-students-stick-stem/602635.

16. *Health Advising.* (n.d.). Xavier University. Retrieved August 19, 2020, from www.xavier.edu/health-advising.

17. Gershenson, S., Hart, C. M., Lindsay, C. A., & Papageorge, N. W. (2017). *The long-run impacts of same-race teachers* (pp. 1–62, Rep. No. 10630). Institute of Labor Economics. www.iza.org/publications/dp/10630; See also Milner, R. H., & Howard, T. (2004). Black teachers, black students, black communities, and brown: Perspectives and insights from experts. *The Journal of Negro Education, 73*(3), 285–297.

18. National Center for Education Statistics. (2019, October). *Bachelor's degrees conferred by postsecondary institutions, by race/ethnicity and sex of student: Selected years, 1976–77 through 2017–18.* https://nces.ed.gov/programs/digest/d19/tables/dt19_322.20.asp.

19. Mitchell, C. Data: The schools named after Confederate figures. (2020, June 17). *Education Week.* www.edweek.org/ew/section/multimedia/data-the-schools-named-after-confederate-figures.html.

20. DiAngelo, R. J. (2018). *White fragility: Why it's so hard for white people to talk about racism.* Beacon Press.

21. Kendi, I. X. (2019). *How to be an antiracist.* One World.

22. Kendi, I. X. (2020, July 1). *Founder's statement.* Retrieved August 31, 2020, from www.bu.edu/antiracism-center/the-center/founder-statement.

23. Muñiz, J. (2019, September 23). *5 ways culturally responsive teaching benefits learners.* New America. Retrieved August 25, 2020, from www.newamerica.org/education-policy/edcentral/5-ways-culturally-responsive-teaching-benefits-learners.

24. Oakes, J., Maier, A., & Daniel, J. (2017). *Community schools: An evidence-based strategy for equitable school improvement.* Learning Policy Institute. https://learningpolicyinstitute.org/product/community-schools-equitable-improvement-brief.

25. Barrett, N., McEachin, A., Mills, J. N., & Valant, J. (2017). *What are the sources of school discipline disparities by student race and family income?* Education Research Alliance. https://educationresearchalliancenola.org/publications

/what-are-the-sources-of-school-discipline-disparities-by-student-race-and
-family-income.

Chapter 11

1. Scafidi, B. (2017). *Back to the staffing surge.* EdChoice. www.edchoice.org
/research/back-staffing-surge.

2. NEA Research. (2019). *Rankings of the states 2018 and estimates of school
statistics 2019.* National Education Association. https://www.nea.org/research
-publications.

3. Raby, J. (2018, March 6). West Virginia leaders reach deal to end 9-day
teachers strike. *PBS News Hour.* www.pbs.org/newshour/nation/west-virginia
-leaders-reach-deal-to-end-9-day-teachers-strike.

4. DeAngelis, C. A. (2020, June 15). *Inflation-adjusted K–12 education spending per student has increased by 280 percent since 1960.* Reason Foundation.
www.reason.org/commentary/inflation-adjusted-k-12-education-spending-per
-student-has-increased-by-280-percent-since-1960.

5. Scafidi, B. (2017). *Back to the staffing surge* (pp. 1–45). EdChoice. www
.edchoice.org/research/back-staffing-surge.

6. Cavanagh, S. (2017, June 20). Most K–12 spending goes to salaries and
benefits. *Education Week.* www.edweek.org/ew/articles/2017/06/21/most-k-12
-spending-goes-to-salaries-and.html

7. Aldeman, C. (2016). *The pension Pac-Man: How pension debt eats away
at teacher salaries.* Bellwether Education Partners. www.teacherpensions.org/sites
/default/files/Teacher%20Pension%20Pac-Man_Web.pdf.

8. Price, S. S., & Sawyer, J. J. (2018, August 15). *Health care update: Addressing the hard choices.* Los Angeles Unified School District Board of Education.
https://boe.lausd.net/sites/default/files/HealthCareUpdateAddressingtheHardChoi
ces.pdf.

9. At the time of writing, the price was $2,000. Due to coronavirus, prices may
have subsequently dropped. See *Rental stats and trends: Los Angeles, CA.* (2019).
www.renthop.com/average-rent-in/los-angeles-ca; *2019–2020 salaries for teachers with regular credentials (T) C Basis.* (2020). Los Angeles Unified School District Board of Education. https://achieve.lausd.net/cms/lib/CA01000043/Centricity
/Domain/280/Salary%20Tables/Salary%2019-20/T%20Table-Annual.pdf.

10. U.S. Bureau of Labor Statistics. (2020, April 10). *Home: Occupational out-
look handbook.* Retrieved August 8, 2020, from www.bls.gov/ooh.

11. Kraft, M. A., & Monti-Nussbaum, M. (May 2020). *The big problem with
little interruptions to classroom learning.* Annenberg, Brown University. www.doi
.org/10.26300/6b7g-nm11.

12. Cavanagh, S. (2017, June 20). Most K–12 spending goes to salaries and
benefits. *Education Week.* www.edweek.org/policy-politics/most-k-12-spending
-goes-to-salaries-and-benefits/2017/06.

13. Association of American Medical Colleges. (n.d.). *Specialty profiles: Careers in medicine.* Retrieved August 8, 2020, from www.aamc.org/cim/explore -options/specialty-profiles.

14. For more, see Hess, F. M. (2019). *Transforming schools requires more than "more is better" reform.* Retrieved September 4, 2020, from National Institute for Excellence in Teaching, www.niet.org/research-and-policy/show/research /transforming-schools-requires-more-than-more-is-better-reform.

Chapter 12

1. Cutler, A. (2020, April 14). *Arlington County School District announces it won't teach any new material.* Fox 5 DC. www.fox5dc.com/news/arlington-county -school-district-announces-it-wont-teach-any-new-material.

2. United Teachers Los Angeles. (2020, April 8). *Sideletter agreement between the Los Angeles Unified School District and United Teachers Los Angeles.* www.utla .net/sites/default/files/utla-lausd_sideletter_for_covid-19_impact_effects_-_final _all_signatures_.pdf.

3. Gross, B., & Opalka, A. (2020, June 10). *Too many schools leave learning to chance during the pandemic.* Center on Reinventing Public Education. www.crpe .org/thelens/too-many-schools-leave-learning-chance-during-pandemic.

4. Shin, D., Lee, H., Lee, G., & Kim, S. (2019). The role of curiosity and interest in learning and motivation. In K. Renninger, & S. Hidi (Authors), *The Cambridge Handbook of Motivation and Learning* (Cambridge Handbooks in Psychology, pp. 443–464). Cambridge University Press. doi:10.1017/9781316823279.020; Sparks, S. D. (2018, May 1). Is curiosity as good at predicting children's reading, math success as self-control? Study says yes. *Inside School Research.* [blog]. https://blogs.edweek.org/edweek/inside-school-research/2018/05/whats_more _important_for_academics_control_curiosity.html.

5. Centers for Disease Control and Prevention. (2020, July 24). *Health equity considerations and racial and ethnic minority groups.* www.cdc.gov/coronavirus /2019-ncov/community/health-equity/race-ethnicity.html.

6. Gross, B., & Opalka, A. (2018). *Too many schools leave learning to chance during the pandemic.* Center on Reinventing Public Education. www.crpe.org /thelens/too-many-schools-leave-learning-chance-during-pandemic; Hess, F. M. (2020, June 24). COVID-19 shutdown: A crash course in problems with schools' over-regulation. *National Review.* www.aei.org/op-eds/covid-19-shutdown-a-crash -course-in-problems-with-schools-over-regulation.

7. Wolfman-Arent, A., & Mezzacappa, D. (2020, March 18). *Philly schools forbid graded "remote instruction" during shutdown for equity concerns.* WHYY. https://whyy.org/articles/philly-schools-forbid-remote-instruction-during-shutdown -for-equity-concerns.

8. Tuchman, S., & McKittrick, L. (2020, May 5). *Federal special education guidance is clear; now states must step up.* Center on Reinventing Public Education.

www.crpe.org/thelens/federal-special-education-guidance-clear-now-states-must
-step.

9. Plachta, A. (2020, March 18). During coronavirus school closures, distance learning may only exacerbate academic inequities. *Los Angeles Daily News.* www.dailynews.com/2020/03/18/during-coronavirus-school-closures-distance
-learning-may-only-exacerbate-academic-inequities.

10. Sawchuk, S., & Samuels, C. A. (2020, April 10). Where are they? Students go missing in shift to remote classes. *Education Week, 39*(40). www.edweek.org
/ew/articles/2020/04/10/where-are-they-students-go-missing-in.html.

11. Koetsier, J. (2020, May 23). 25 million students on COVID-19: "Depression, anxiety and loneliness" hitting peak levels. *Forbes.* www.forbes.com/sites
/johnkoetsier/2020/05/23/25-million-students-on-covid-19-depression-anxiety
-and-loneliness-hitting-peak-levels/#71718a6377b8.

12. Blume, H. (2020). L.A. school district confronts $200 million in coronavirus costs and a grim budget future. *Los Angeles Times.* www.latimes.com
/california/story/2020-04-20/lausd-faced-with-200-million-in-underfunded
-expenses-due-to-coronavirus-outbreak.

Chapter 13

1. Noguera, P. (2014, June 18). In defense of teacher tenure. *Wall Street Journal.* www.wsj.com/articles/pedro-noguera-in-defense-of-teacher-tenure-1403134951.

2. Yeats, W. B. (1919). The second coming [Poem]. www.poetryfoundation.org
/poems/43290/the-second-coming.

3. Beyond Conflict. (2020). *America's divided mind: Understanding the psychology that drives us apart.* www.beyondconflictint.org/wp-content/uploads/2020
/06/Beyond-Conflict-America_s-Div-ided-Mind-JUNE-2020-FOR-WEB.pdf.

4. Mattis, J. (2019, December). The enemy within. *The Atlantic.* www.the
atlantic.com/magazine/archive/2019/12/james-mattis-the-enemy-within/600781.

5. Arthur Brooks' keynote speech at 2020 National Prayer Breakfast. (2020, February 6). C-SPAN. www.c-span.org/video/?c4853101/arthur-brooks-keynote
-speech-2020-national-prayer-breakfast.

6. Brooks, A. C. (2020). Trump and I disagreed at the National Prayer Breakfast. But we listened to each other. *Washington Post.* www.washingtonpost.com
/opinions/trump-and-i-disagreed-at-the-national-prayer-breakfast-but-we-listened
-to-each-other/2020/02/14/ae8d019c-4f40-11ea-9b5c-eac5b16dafaa_story.html.

Index

About the Authors

Rick Hess is director of education policy studies at the American Enterprise Institute. He pens *Education Week*'s popular blog "Rick Hess Straight Up," is a senior contributor to *Forbes*, and serves as executive editor of *Education Next*. His books include *Letters to a Young Education Reformer, Cage-Busting Leadership, The Cage-Busting Teacher, The Same Thing Over and Over, Common Sense School Reform*, and *Spinning Wheels*. Rick's work has appeared in scholarly outlets including *Harvard Education Review, American Politics Quarterly, Social Science Quarterly, Teachers College Record*, and *Urban Affairs Review*. He is a regular presence on radio and TV and writes about education for popular publications like *The New York Times, USA Today, The Wall Street Journal, Newsweek*, and *The Washington Post*. He's the senior founding fellow for the Leadership Institute of Nevada and serves on the boards of directors of the National Association of Charter School Authorizers and 4.0 Schools. Rick started his career teaching high school social studies in Baton Rouge, Louisiana, and has since taught at the University of Virginia, the University of Pennsylvania, Georgetown University, Rice University, Johns Hopkins University, and Harvard University. He holds his PhD in government and MEd in teaching and curriculum from Harvard University.

Pedro Noguera is dean of the University of Southern California Rossier School of Education. His books include *Unfinished Business: Closing the Racial Achievement Gap in Our Nation's Schools; The Trouble with Black Boys . . . and Other Reflections on Race, Equity, and the Future of Public Education; City Schools and the American Dream*; and *Race, Equity, and Education: Sixty Years from* Brown, with Jill Pierce and Roey Ahram. Pedro serves on the boards of numerous national and local organizations, and regularly comments on educational issues for national news outlets including CNN, *The New York Times*, *The Los Angeles Times*, and NPR. He has received numerous awards for his research and advocacy efforts aimed at fighting poverty, and was elected to the National Academy of Education in 2014. After starting out as a social studies teacher in Providence, Rhode Island, and Oakland, California, Pedro has since taught at New York University, the Harvard Graduate School of Education, the University of California, Berkeley, and the University of California, Los Angeles. He has a PhD in sociology from the University of California, Berkeley, and an MA in sociology from Brown University.